# THE SURVIVORS

*Five Stories of Depression
& Manic-Depression*

By Bob Hill

Edited by Jena Monahan

Published by
The Manic Depressive
and Depressive Association
of Louisville, Inc.

The Survivors: Five Stories
of Depression & Manic-
Depression

Written by Bob Hill

Edited by Jena Monahan

Funded by a grant from The
Mary and Barry Bingham Sr.
Fund

Design & production by
Moonlight Graphic Works /
Stephen Sebree

Photographs by Pam
Spaulding

Published by The Manic
Depressive and Depressive
Association of Louisville, Inc.
P. O. Box 7315
Louisville, Kentucky 40257-
0315

Printed by The Merrick
Printing Company Inc.

ISBN 0-9621352-9-1

# PREFACE

This is a book about five people who are depressive or manic-depressive. It is not about medicine. It is not about miracle cures. It is simply an attempt to explain how mental illness has affected their lives, and the lives of those around them.

They are very real people: a bank teller, a housewife, a seminary student, a printer and a salesman. They are the people next door, or perhaps the people in your family.

They have shared their most intimate moments in hopes that others will see that the first steps to recovery from mental illness are recognition and understanding.

They know too well of the victories, defeats and uncertainties of their disease. They know that with love, faith and support it is possible to lead a full and productive life.

It took a tremendous amount of courage for them to speak. All they ask in return is that you listen.

Bob Hill

Bob Hill has been a reporter, columnist and feature writer for the Louisville Times and Courier-Journal for 15 years

I t is always encouraging to encounter someone who has known the exuberance of Frank Marx and his great desire to assist others in realizing their potential and living productive and valuable lives.

I came to know Frank Marx through his efforts to establish a halfway house for those burdened with depression and manic-depression. He so wants others to know the possibilities for living that his own exuberance needs to be bounded by his friends. He is aware of this and is always seeking others to help complement his own ideas.

This dream of establishing such a halfway house is typical of Frank Marx's desire to help a part of society live up to its potential. Knowing the burdens of such an affliction himself, he also knows how society often ostracizes such people. This only increases their frustrations and deepens the roots of the disorders. But Frank has the experience of knowing the support of others and knowing that these persons can continue to live very productive and valuable lives. For that to happen, there is always need for those first steps, and a halfway house would certainly provide such steps and the people to offer the encouragement and the caution that is needed to bring the expansive desires for life into focus. It is all just a simple example of that interrelatedness and interdependence that makes our society and culture viable. As a people we have come a long way with our efforts to integrate various sectors of society into the mainstream of life. But there is always more to be done.

We are tempted to be discouraged by the many obvious burdens in our midst, the addictions that close in so many lives, the violence that is often the result or the cause of such addictions. We should acknowledge the people who are endeavoring to encourage others to live valuable lives.

We hope and pray for the support of this project, recognizing that by it society will be made that much stronger and that we will see in our midst the working of Gospel values and something of the reign of God growing to fruition.

Sincerely in Christ,
(Rt. Rev.) Timothy Kelly, Abbot of Gethsemani

# DEDICATION

The Manic Depressive and Depressive Association of Louisville, Inc. is very grateful to the Mary and Barry Bingham Sr. Fund for the grant that made this book possible.

# CONTENTS

*Chapter One*

# MARTHA COLSTON

*"I just sit wondering if or when the bomb will go off. I can remember pleading with God to take me out of my misery, and then I can remember thinking that I was God and I could put myself out of my misery. I can remember begging to get off the roller coaster. . ."*

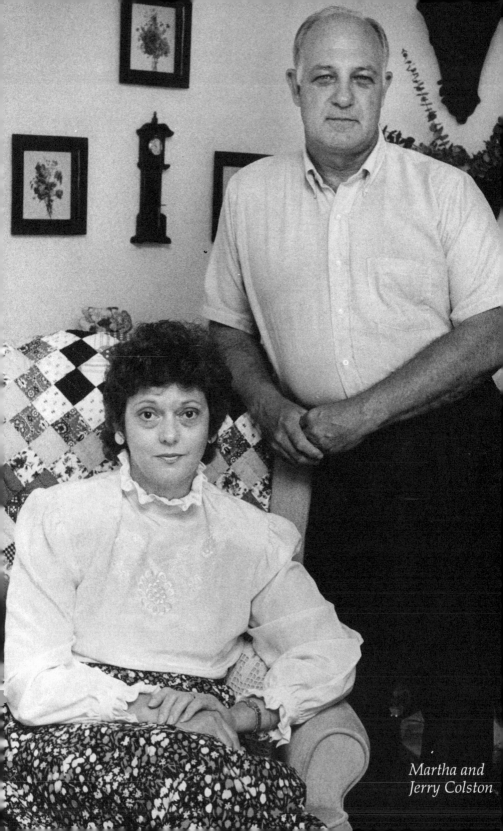

*Martha and
Jerry Colston*

As part of the therapy to deal with her illness, Martha Colston kept a diary of her feelings in a pink spiral notebook. Some of the writing was sketchy, with words crossed out or lines drawn from one paragraph to another as she struggled to put her feelings in order.

Thoughts do not always come in sequence for a manic-depressive. Conscious control is impossible. Feelings can flare and race away, then plunge the manic-depressive into darkness. Manic-depressives can become numb to the outside world, then very sensitive to it.

Martha Colston wrote about that darkness and those sensitivities. She said it is like being in a cave:

"I took a trip through Mammoth Cave once. When we got in the middle of a huge cavern we were asked to sit down and rest. The guide extinguished the lights and told us to remain silent. She wanted us to feel the way early explorers felt alone in a dark cave.

"There was not a single drop of light. It was pitch dark, cold, clammy and eerie. Now and then I could hear a drop of water, or something that sounded like a mouse running and squealing. We sat anxiously as silence settled in and then we could hear the guide strike a match. For one brief moment there was light again, and people sitting next to me, and I wasn't alone after all.

"As the light dimmed, the darkness and silence closed in again. The guide dropped the match to the floor and in that dark cavern it made a noise that sounded like a thud. Outside of that huge cavern in Mammoth Cave, depression is the loneliest and darkest you will ever feel."

Still looking for an example that others could feel and understand, she wrote again of depression on the next page in her spiral notebook, immersing herself in the imagery of her illness:

"One morning before sunrise I missed my ride to help set up breakfast for a group on church retreat. I didn't let that stop me. I set out in the dark on a wooded gravel road. I was well on my way before I realized I was in total darkness in the woods with only the moon reflecting off the gravel to guide my feet. I walked one step at a time. I began to hear every noise imaginable; hoot owls, breaking branches, leaves rustling in the wind, the sound of something moving closer.

"I felt there must be bats flying around my head, and I was sure there was a rattlesnake on my path. I stepped in more than one rut, turned my ankle and thought of screaming bloody murder, but I was alone; who would have heard me?

"I was terrified, but I was too far along the road to go back and still a long way from my destination. I prayed to God for safety, to live and see the sunrise. I did make it, and as I was walking through the cafeteria door the sun was coming up and it seemed to me that's what depression is like; it's always darkest before the dawn."

All too frequently Martha Colston, 51, must fight her illness in the dark. She has been hospitalized three times in recent years for depressive and manic-depressive episodes, episodes — like those of so many other people — that were complicated by misdiagnoses as well as a longtime thyroid problem.

Her hospitalizations, struggles within her family, and more recently her problems with insurance companies over bills for her treatment, are fresh in her mind.

"Actually," she said, "I don't know when my life was ever calm. I am still asking myself: When does the fun begin?"

Certainly her early life was difficult. She was born in Richmond, Va., one of two daughters. Her father, a mechanical engineer, was an alcoholic, a problem that would haunt her in family relationships.

"I can't remember a day of my life that didn't have drinking in it," she said.

Her parents fought over her father's drinking. Her mother wanted a divorce, so her father took Martha away and hid her with an aunt.

"I think my mother thought it would be better if she lived with my father rather than have that happen, so they got back together," Martha said. "They told me they went back together for me."

Martha's father was transferred to Louisville when she was 9. Her dreams were to travel, to be an archaeologist or an airline stewardess, or perhaps sing and dance and entertain.

The dreams did not last long. When she was 12 she became ill with an overactive thyroid, a rare problem for an adolescent. She was very sensitive to the few drugs then available. Ultimately, she spent summers in bed for five years, from age 12 to about 17. It was a miserable time.

"I was tired all the time. My pulse was 120. I missed 42 days of school when I was a sophomore. I went to the doctor three times a week. He knew the problem was my thyroid, but they didn't have anything to treat me. They put me to bed so I wouldn't drop dead on them.

"I was very lonely. People came for a while, and then they didn't come anymore. I'd go to school and make a friend, and then they would jerk me out of school and that friend would be gone. It was not too pleasant."

Her recreation was to place a big folding table across

her lap and work jigsaw puzzles. She was slow to develop physically and didn't have much opportunity to develop social skills.

"Everybody else was downstairs. I can remember thinking I shouldn't have to stay in bed. I really didn't feel that
badly. My father was a very strict disciplinarian, and he
wouldn't allow any of the guys to visit me in my bedroom even though everyone was around.

"I got out some, but my activities were always limited. I
was allowed to go to the pool and sit, but I was not
allowed to swim. That was the doctor's orders, not my
mother's."

Martha's difficult adolescence was compounded by her
father's drinking. He could be a charming, friendly man
— a true Southern gentleman — but he could also be verbally abusive to his daughters. Her mother, who was
depressive, was also verbally abusive. Her mother's family hailed from England and had much of the famous
British reserve. They had difficulty communicating real
feelings.

So it was no surprise that when an opportunity to leave
home showed up, Martha grabbed it.

"I met this young man at the swimming pool, and we
started dating. We dated for a year, and my father decided it was not a good idea. We hadn't done anything, but
my father decided I couldn't see him again. He just didn't
like him."

Martha's boyfriend joined the service. When he came
home on leave he kept pushing her to get married. Finally, she quit high school in her senior year and married
him.

Aside from his pleas, there was a tragic incident in her
life that helped push her out of an already bad family sit-

uation.

"One of the truly pivotal points in my life was when I was 16 and my best friend drowned. After all these years I still haven't recovered from losing that sweet, gentle spirit.

"She had epilepsy, but I wasn't told about it because of the stigma. She stepped into a pool on Labor Day weekend and drowned. I would have been with her, but I had out-of-town company. I blamed myself for not being there.

"Then I decided after being ill myself and losing my young friend, that life was too short to live in a family situation clouded with alcohol. I married and left."

The young couple moved to New Jersey, where Martha's husband was stationed. Martha tried to finish high school but became pregnant and had to quit. She later got her degree at night school.

The marriage lasted four difficult years, ending in divorce.

"Guess where I was?" Martha said. "I had two children and was divorced at 21 and back living with my parents. My father had a heart attack not long after I moved back in. I blamed myself. Everything that ever happened in my family I felt was my fault."

Soon after Martha moved back home her mother sued her father for divorce, leaving Martha to help care for her father while he recovered. She also worked outside the home at a retail store and as a bank teller.

"I had to go home. I couldn't go anywhere else. For all his problems, my father was the only nurturing parent I had, so I had to stay. I stayed there for five years with him."

She had experienced many mood swings during her

adolescence and marriage, but none that threw her into strong highs or lows. She didn't recognize the swings as any kind of mental illness; she thought that was the way life was supposed to be. When she was in her 20s she began having what she called "anguish" attacks that continued for almost 25 years.

"They start at the base of the brain, and the anguish just builds and builds and builds until you think you're head is going to explode.

"It's not just a headache, but it's a pain that pushes and pushes against the side of your head like a balloon until you feel it will explode. It started with stress, a certain problem or situation that I couldn't get off my mind. It would eventually subside, but sometimes I would yell and want to go someplace and scream. Sometimes I would go into the bedroom and scream into a pillow.

"I just thought it was the pressure of trying to raise the children and work and take care of them. I thought that was what was wrong with me. I never thought of anything beyond that.

"You have to understand that I have been very hard to diagnose because I was told as a young person that you do not get depressed. You put on a happy face. You get dressed, go out and carry on. So the doctor has a terrible time breaking through that.

"I didn't know what was happening to me. I didn't know it wasn't normal. What's normal?"

There was one brief period in her 20s when Martha found a little relief. She began swimming often, which seemed to help reduce the tension, and she went to a doctor who began treating her for hypoglycemia — low blood sugar.

"For some reason it helped. It was just a special diet, and

I saw the doctor once a month. He was so kind to me. But I wouldn't have sought out a psychiatrist or anything. That was before the time when you really went to a psychiatrist."

Martha's split from her mother didn't last. Her mother had moved to Virginia after divorcing Martha's father, but eventually returned to Louisville. For about a year she and Martha lived together; they both had financial problems and needed to share expenses.

It was during that time that Martha married Jerry Colston, an old family friend whom she had been dating for about five years. They had begun dating about the time Martha's father suffered his heart attack.

Jerry, who worked in sales most of his life, had been getting along very well with Martha's two children. He'd also come from a family split by divorce and understood some of the problems it generates.

Part of the reason they waited five years to marry was that Jerry's mother was a widow, and he helped with his family. He, too, felt that Martha's anxiety attacks were related to family stress rather than a mental illness.

"I never picked out anything while we were dating," he said. "I just felt it was somewhat normal. I grew up in an unhappy background too."

Even though they had dated for years, Martha was still uncertain about marriage.

"I wasn't sure I would ever get married again," Martha said. "I just didn't like it the first time, and I didn't want to do that again. I didn't know I'd get married until the day I got married. I honestly didn't know if I would make it to the church or not."

They were married on June 23, 1967, and eventually had a son of their own.

Their family relationship hemorrhaged badly in the mid-1970s when Martha's oldest son developed problems of his own.

The Colstons believe many of his problems were brought on by the trauma of court-ordered busing to desegregate the Jefferson County schools. Their son had to leave his home school and friends in his junior year to go to another school. He became hostile and depressed. He sought treatment at a center in Minnesota. He joined the Navy, had to leave because of his problems, then rejoined. There were some periods of communication, but the degenerating relationship between Martha and her son carried over into the 1980s. For the last three years there has been no contact.

Martha, trying to fight increasing depression while her family was breaking apart, began meeting with a therapist. Her therapist suggested she see a psychiatrist. At the same time — about 1987 — her family doctor began treating her recurring thyroid condition.

Soon she was taking drugs for depression, anxiety, an ulcer and pain, many of them prescribed by her general practitioner. The family stress, her sometimes stressful job as a bank teller, the medications, the family problems kept building until Martha reached a point where she began losing her concentration. Her thoughts were fragmented. She was unable to complete a sentence.

The flood of emotion broke following an incident at work involving her cash drawer.

She was considered a very competent bank teller with an excellent work record, but one night, due to all the pressures, she had become sick and nauseous. In her haste to get home she forgot to put away her cash drawer. There was nothing criminal about the incident — someone else placed the cash drawer in the vault for her — but she was reprimanded and placed on six months' probation.

She tried to work the six months, but the pressure was too much; she broke down physically and emotionally.

"I had an appointment with my doctor," she said. "I told him, 'I can't think. I'm having fragmented thoughts. I can't finish a thought.' My doctor called my psychiatrist, and he called my therapist. I went down at 8 o'clock one night to see her and handed her the bag of all the drugs I had been taking. She called the psychiatrist and said I was so high on drugs she was afraid to let me go home. She said I needed to go to the hospital."

Martha's admittance to a mental hospital — after all the years of stress, pressure and guilt — proved to be a wonderful release. She no longer had to immerse herself in the lives of so many other people; suddenly she was surrounded by people who only wanted to help her. She slept for 16 hours her first day in the hospital.

"I knew why I was there. I was so ill because I was so high on drugs. I was glad to be in a place where they were going to take care of me. The majority of the people that go there for the first time are amazed at what the hospital is like, and wonder why they haven't been there before, or why they didn't want to come. It's just a wonderful experience."

Being hospitalized, of course, is not a wonderful experience for everyone. Even Martha had a few problems initially. Her regular psychiatrist left on vacation, and Martha saw five different doctors over a five-day period, none of whom seemed to communicate with her very well.

Her family also kept pressing for a quick diagnosis of

her problem. The answer she received was "major depression"; incorrect, but understandable given her symptoms.

But mostly her first experience with being hospitalized
for mental illness was very positive, as she would write in
her pink spiral notebook later:

"Family and friends are at a loss when a loved one is
admitted to a psychiatric hospital. The doors are shut and
locked, and many people find that frightening. For the
majority of patients the doors are locked for the privacy
and protection of the patient. Chemical imbalances in the
brain can cause suicidal thoughts and attempts, and the
hospital is a place of comfort and protection. Many
patients need privacy from family members, including
abusive spouses and lovers.

"Contrary to popular opinion, the rooms are not padded
cells but are just like any other double-occupancy hospital
room, except there is no telephone and no television.

"Your feet hit the floor just as soon as possible. By 7 a.m.
you begin a grueling schedule of classes, interviews with
doctors, nurses and social workers, recreational activities,
medication, crafts and art therapy until 10 p.m. when you
can fall into bed. Some hardy souls stay up much later in
the day room playing cards and watching television.

"These exercises are scheduled at the discretion of the
patient's doctor. The sooner the patient becomes
involved, the sooner the patient leaves."

So Martha soon learned the basic truth of the hospital.
Her doctor would see her almost every day for 10 to 15
minutes and deal with her medication. She was assigned
a primary nurse who spent time with her every day. For
all that, most of the hands-on support and healing
occurred as the patients reached out to each other.

Most of these relationships were built during an activity

called "community," a time when all the patients on the same floor would gather in chairs in a circle and talk.

"We had 23 people," she said. "It's a time to talk about our gripes, or about the things that make us happy; just what you would talk about at family mealtime.

"We spent a lot of time together and a lot of time helping one another. We'd say hello to the new people. We'd say goodbye to those going home. We'd talk about why we didn't have popcorn with butter on it the night before.

"We'd talk about how we wished they would clean the bathrooms better. It was about what you would talk about at home. What happens is you have very, very intimate relationships in the hospital."

The doctors come by after community, and the nurses — who wear civilian clothes — monitor it, but mostly it's the patients who keep the community going. It's group therapy, sometimes chatty, sometimes fun, sometimes tearful. It builds an emotional bond between patients that often only exists for the time they are in the hospital; the patients may know too much about one another to want to meet outside the hospital.

But sometimes the bonds do carry over, and the patients will meet in each other's homes. Or they will send cards to the friends they left behind. Martha often sent such cards. One day she received a letter from a friend just out of the hospital that said, in part:

"I just wanted you to know that I loved and appreciated your card. You are right. We are very special people and just doing little things like sending a card can mean more to a person than the most expensive gift on earth."

Her friend went on to write that once, while in the hospital, she had a radio station dedicate the song "Lean on Me" to her friends. They all gathered in the community

room  and held hands while listening to it. Many of them
cried. Martha's friend did not — at least not that time.

"My last day there," her friend wrote, "the group got
together and dedicated the same song to me. It came over
the radio as a very special dedication, and again everyone
was in the room was holding hands and singing. This
time I could not hold back the tears.

"Martha, I have never in my life felt so loved and so
cared about.  It just shows that if you take a little time to
tell someone you are thinking about them and that you
care, you will get the same special thought and feeling 10
times over."

Martha said those intimate moments in community —
at least the morning sessions — were often followed by
brief private conversations between patients and their
doctors. Then the patients would be given their medication, perhaps do some light exercise, make crafts, then go
to lunch.

"There were definitely patients with more severe symptoms than I had," she said. "Some were having shock
treatments. Some were very depressed and wouldn't
come out of their rooms except to go to meals."

In the afternoons she had specific classes scheduled by
her doctors, classes on stress, assertiveness and perhaps
self-concept. They were aimed at drawing her out, trying
to get her to express her feelings.  She wrote about her
problems in her spiral notebook:

How I Can Depend on Myself
Taking responsibility for myself — I depend on Jerry
way too much for my well-being.

Making decisions that concern me — start small.

Perhaps my expectations are too great — be realistic.

Do not feel guilty when not able to keep commitments. When making commitments, explain the situation.

Don't overload — don't bite off more than I can chew.

Learn to live one day at a time — or one minute at a time.

"I think assertiveness was probably one of my favorites," she said. "Most of us didn't know we could have feelings, that many feelings. You just don't realize. Assertiveness helps you to express your feelings in a way acceptable to people."

After the more intense afternoon classes, many of the patients relaxed a little in art-therapy classes. After that would come an evening meal, then perhaps a dance, swimming, another community meeting, television and bed.

The stay in the hospital didn't dull Martha's sharp sense of humor. She and the other patients would sometimes order pizza over the phone and delight in imagining the reaction when some deliveryman was told to take the pizza to a mental hospital.

As Martha improved, as the daily sessions with her psychiatrist became more helpful, her doctor changed her class schedule and her medicine. She had come into the hospital taking heavy doses of a variety of drugs. Gradually, they were reduced to one anti-depressant. She was in the hospital 43 days, from July 1987 until early September. When she was released she was feeling better but still had no real understanding of her illness. She didn't feel she had any goals in life.

"I felt like I never got an answer to anything. My personal opinion was my doctor thought the more I knew the worse I would feel."

Nor did she want to go home.

"I was comfortable. I was with friends. I just didn't want to go."

But she went home. She had to. She began seeing her therapist once a week. They talked about options and goals, of looking out toward a specific point and then reaching it.

Her anti-depressant medicine wasn't working, so she switched to another drug. She went to a wellness clinic to learn relaxation techniques. She tried biofeedback, sitting in a lounge chair with sensors attached to her body to determine where she was most stressed.

None of it worked. Fueled by the medicine, she was beginning to feel manic.

"Here I am, I'm starting to elevate, and I'm getting real crazy. I mean, when I get manic I get very spiritual. I had been having this wonderful relationship with God, but it was getting better and better. I thought I was super. I thought I was just great."

At the time, she had begun going to support-group meetings three nights a week. She picked out a man who had said at the meetings that he had no concept of God. She spent the next three months trying to give him one. It's a situation she laughs about in retrospect.

"The whole idea was that he was going to know about God before I got through with him. I harassed him. I honestly harassed him. I dropped notes where he worked. I just kept after him. It was embarrassing when you think back on it."

While on her high, she remembers being the "clown for Christ" during a church retreat, carrying on, laughing, joking and being everywhere at once. Often during her manic stages she would "collect friends," going shopping with them, or to lunch, and spending hours on the telephone.

While manic, thoughts would race through her mind, chasing each other, but never quite making contact. In time those highs would be followed by lows. The cycles continued; she could not control them.

"I'm telling you I would walk into a room for a half-hour, and I would be up, and walk out and be flat. Up and down, up and down."

While manic, Martha began drinking large glasses of wine in the evenings to help her get to sleep. She also told her husband she wanted a divorce; she was going to be independent and take care of herself because she felt she could do anything.

Jerry accepted her threats as part of her mood swings; he would talk to her about it but never took the conversations too seriously.

"But I would have if I thought she had really been serious," he said. "The thing is we could be carrying on a conversation, and she'd walk into the other room and you'd go in and get ready to start talking to her and you couldn't see past her eyeballs. She was absolutely past conversation. It's like turning off a light switch.

"I didn't know who I was going to be talking to. Her attitude, her personality, her ability to respond, it would change in 20 minutes."

Martha went to her therapist looking for help to get off the roller coaster. She didn't find it. Disappointed, she went home and was watching a television show about the brain. The subject matter was manic-depression.

"I looked at Jerry and I said, 'That's what I've got. I know that's what I've got.' "

She was right. She went to her doctor, and he agreed with her. Because she hadn't exhibited a serious manic state prior to that, she did not blame him for missing the diagnosis.

"I went in the hospital the second time in November 1988," she said. "I remember because I was in for Thanksgiving."

She was only in the hospital a short time when she dropped into a deep depression. She had suicidal thoughts. She even considered acting on them, but never did.

"It was just black. All around me. I'll tell you what was really confusing to me was God was gone. I told my doctor; I said, 'God promised to be with me and he's not with me. If I can't have God, I don't want to live. You can lock me up here. You can lock me up at home. You can lock me up in my bedroom. But just as soon as I can I'm going to take a bottle of pills.' It was hell."

Back in the same hospital where she had been before, Martha was placed in a "guided group," a group that was only to talk about the present, not the past or the future.

Its purpose was to draw out the patients, to have them talk only of immediate feelings. Martha disliked attending; she was never comfortable talking about her feelings.

One day she was given a list of human emotions or characteristics to help her better identify what she had been feeling. She checked off 23 of them, bashful, interested, optimistic, determined, frustrated and frightened among them.

Some days there were only four people in her group. If a patient walked out rather than speak, the others would talk about their feelings about the person leaving the group. Guided groups could be very intense. Many of the patients, forced to confront their emotions, could only sit and cry.

"I'll tell you the truth," said Martha, "the first time I went through the group we sat for 40 minutes and didn't say a word. The group leaders kept asking if we were comfortable with the silence and we said, 'Yes.' "

Martha later wrote about her manic-depression in her notebook:

"What is the one feeling that describes my manic-depression? Confusion! I stay in a state of confusion. I see myself seated on a time bomb in a state of confusion.

"Most people would run like hell. I just sit wondering if or when the bomb will go off. I can remember pleading with God to take me out of my misery, and then I can remember thinking that I was God and I could put myself out of my misery. I can remember begging to get off the roller coaster, and then I was hurled into pitch-black darkness.

"I remember laying wide awake one night, and the next morning it seemed so strange that I didn't even shut my eyes. I felt great."

She was in the hospital 23 days, again going through the familiar patterns of community, self-improvement classes, art therapy, exercises and sessions with her nurse and doctor. She'd been given blood tests during her stay, and for the first time lithium was prescribed. It helped, but she was still feeling a little depressed when she went home, not at all ready for the sometimes forced gaiety of Christmas.

"It was so bad," said Jerry, "that we had to leave town. During that same period I lost my brother and our sister-in-law died. Martha was in tremendous grief, and it sort of kept her down. I would say it was spring before she really made any headway.

"It was hard. It makes you confusèd. It makes you frustrated and cynical."

Martha's manic-depression and Jerry's frustration sometimes made communication difficult with their youngest son.  Her doctor knew she was not feeling well, but the only answer seemed to be to give the lithium — and the anti-depressant — time to work.

Her medicines never balanced. She never felt well. Last December she was given a new drug that could only be taken on a very strict diet; she could have no aged cheese, meat, alcohol, bananas or caffeine.

"If I ate the wrong foods with this medicine," she said, "I could have a stroke and die."

The new medicine didn't work either. Martha's head remained clouded. She was mildly depressed much of the time. She took a college class, taking notes that made little sense, having to repeat things over and over. She developed what she called "amnesia"; she would be going someplace and become lost, forgetting where she had been or where she was going.

In the summer of 1990 she went back into the hospital again, supposedly for a few tests, and stayed 21 days. She was given a brain scan and all kinds of blood work. Her doctors learned that she had an overactive thyroid, a condition that may have been present for several years.

"I had been to an endocrinologist three years previously, and he had dropped my medication for an overactive thyroid," she said. "It could have started anytime. It could have been bouncing up and down all those years. It could have just started. I don't know."

The Colstons are upset by this. They think that if Martha's thyroid condition had been detected during the first two hospitalizations, it could have saved them a lot of time, grief and money. The money is very important because their group insurance is nearly exhausted.

Insurance is a major worry for many mentally ill people because many have coverage that limits them to only $25,000 lifetime, and hospital stays can easily be $500 a day.

It's common for group coverage for a physical illness to be $1 million lifetime but not for mental illness. Manic-depressives believe that because their illness is a disease of the brain, they should also be entitled to the higher coverage.

"But I'm not that mad at the insurance companies," Jerry said. "I'm no madder at them than I am at the doctors and hospitals that screw up and constantly don't push for an end result for the patient.

"It's a delicate thing, and it's because of the high cost and misreading of patients, and the long periods of stays, that has forced the insurance companies to rebel against the hospitals and doctors. The patient is caught in the middle.

"The answer is better coverage. We can't expect the state of Kentucky to pick up our hospital bills when we think we've got the ability to pay for group insurance. We should have the right to buy it."

Many mental patients worry about medical insurance; it is a constant subject of conversation in the hospitals. The Colstons have done some lobbying with a state legislator, but for the immediate future they are facing severe finan-

cial problems due to Martha's medical expenses. They are
frustrated — and angry — about facing a future with
inadequate insurance when they had been willing all
along to pay group rates to receive it.

It's also hard to maintain a social life — although old
friends and church members often call and ask about
them — because of the uncertainties of Martha's illness.
The Colstons don't go out as often and old friends are not
quite  sure what to say when they see Martha.

By late summer 1990, Martha was taking lithium plus a
mix of three or four other drugs for her thyroid, to help
her sleep and to fight depression. Her life was still a little
out of balance.

"Balance is the key to everything," she said. "When I
take medication for an overactive thyroid, what that can
do is cause me to be depressed from my manic-depression. One can trigger the other.

"This is not an easy time. What can I do? I hope for the
best. We get down to living one day at a time, one minute
at a time, one second at a time. You don't know how you
are going to feel. I might feel just great right now and turn
around, and the bottom will fall out. It's devastating."

After her third stay in the hospital, Martha wrote about
trying to explain her illness to other people. She wrote:

"Many people throughout the last four years have asked
me about my illness, manic-depression, or as the medical
community prefers to call it, bipolar affective disorder.

"Although everyone at some time in their lives will no
doubt experience depression, people seem at a loss as to
what to say, and do not fully understand the illness.
Please do not feel bad; most of us don't understand either.

"I know you would like to help, and I thought the time
had come to give you some insights to a devastating ill-

ness. I wouldn't have done it if I didn't think it would help other people. I hope it helps someone else."

*Chapter Two*

# ANNE FOWLER

*"I would climb up the steps from the basement and there would be all this dirt. That's where I would crawl up and hide. I was about 10 years old, and I was hiding from the world. I'd sit there and rock. I never could cry."*

For almost all of her life Anne Fowler has lived under the heavy blanket of mental depression. As a small child her black moods were so strong she would climb a tree in a thunderstorm, hoping to get struck by lightning. When she was 10 she would hide in the family basement, needing its darkness and solitude. She never had the self-esteem she needed to help her fight her demons.

"My childhood," she said, "was a tragedy of mammoth proportions. I had an insatiable appetite of hatred for myself. I felt all the pain and trouble in the home was my fault. These feelings raced around inside of me until my whole being became a whirlpool of agony."

As a young woman, struggling with what she and her husband admit has often been a difficult marriage, she suffered long bouts of depression.

When she was in her 50s, with her five children grown and out of the house, Anne Fowler would get so depressed she would stay in her dark basement for months at a time, completing a circle that had begun as a child.

At times the blanket has lifted, giving her a glimpse of distant sunlight. She has been most comfortable when caring for others — her relatives, children, husband and mother, the latter an invalid who requires constant attention. When there was no one else to care for — to occupy her attention — her depressions often returned.

Anne Fowler is 63, and the cycles of her life have been repeated over and over and over again. Yet she has never sought professional help for any length of time. Like many people she didn't feel she could afford help, even the help that was available through public agencies. She said the times she did seek psychiatric help it did little good, so she has no confidence in its methods.

Anne is an intelligent, sensitive, likable woman who describes the hell she has been through in phrases that are as sad and clear as they are poetic. She is hanging on, but even now, she has no idea where her life is leading.

"That's the truly sad part," she said. "I think you journalists have a great job. You know what you want. You know where you want to go. You know where you've been. I'm 63 years old and in very poor health. What's left for me? I don't even know where I've been."

Anne Fowler grew up in West Louisville. She lived in a big house on Southwestern Parkway with her mother, her grandmother, her aunt, an uncle and seven nieces and nephews.

Her father was in and out of her life, and their relationship was difficult and traumatic. Her mother was often in Lexington visiting her father, and Anne's life was controlled by members of her immediate family. Several family members drank heavily, adding to the trauma.

"I don't think I was ever a happy child," Anne said. "There was so much distortion in my home life. My mother went off to see my father for months. My grandmother was very stressed. I wasn't able to ride a bicycle, and I was never able to wear shorts. My grandmother said it just wasn't ladylike. My childhood was 24 hours a day of uninterrupted pain."

Anne remembers a lot of the little things about her childhood, the accumulation of hurts that children often carry into adulthood.

Often, especially when blamed for problems she did not cause, she would retreat to a small dirt cellar off the house basement.

"I would climb up the steps from the basement and there would be all this dirt. That's where I would crawl up and hide. I was about 10 years old, and I was hiding from the world. I'd sit in there and rock. I never could cry. I can't really cry now. It would be better if I could cry.

"I was somewhere just recently talking about that cellar and that terrible, musty old smell came back to me. I didn't want anybody to know I was down there. It was my world — my own little secret world down there.

"I stayed in the basement and hid as much as I could. After awhile I learned that whatever my guardian said I did, I would accept the blame for it. Then I would get less punishment."

Problems within her family forced Anne to drop out of school when she was about 13. For a time she worked in a bakery, but then she returned home to work in the house.

"I had a lot of chores to do around the house. And they had a child with cerebral palsy in the family, and I helped take care of him. I was responsible for him a lot. It was something to do. I loved him and he loved me.

"But I felt cheated. I loved school and I was good in school. So I stayed home and I would read a lot."

She met boys, but before she could date anyone seriously he had to meet with her grandmother's approval.

"I was allowed only to go out with Catholic boys," she said. "World War II was going on then, and there were always some boys around. When they came over to the house we would have to gather around the table and say the Rosary. If they didn't know what the Rosary was, out they went. So I learned never to bring in a boy unless he was Catholic. Then I never brought anybody home. It was too embarrassing."

She met Charles Richard Fowler in downtown Louisville toward the end of World War II. Charles, a gregarious, plain-spoken man, was a Marine home on leave.

Anne said the first time she saw him he was in his dress uniform, and she thought he was in the Salvation Army. They quickly hit it off and began kidding each other with harmless banter. They began to date. Charles, a Catholic, knew the Rosary and passed the family test.

"And my grandmother liked him," Anne said.

When he returned to duty, the two wrote each other. When the war ended, they became serious.

"When he got out I wanted to get married," Anne said. "I thought I loved him. I just wanted to get out of the hell-hole."

They dated for a while, then were married.

"Charles wasn't quite ready for marriage right away," she said. "He was one to live for today, the hell with tomorrow. He was drinking at the time, although I really didn't realize it.

"He was from a very, very poor family. When I told him my story, he said, 'I don't care about that.' He said, 'I'm marrying you.' And he was crazy about my mother. She had a very dynamic personality. To me Charles was great and grand and full of life and cheerful. He accepted me for what I was, and that was great."

They were married in 1946. At first they ran off to Lexington to complete their vows but didn't do it. Anne's mother went to Lexington and brought them back to Louisville; they were married in a room in the back of the church.

They have survived 44 years of a difficult, sometimes abusive marriage. There have been long periods when Charles was not home. At other times it was Anne who disappeared — into her depressions and into her basement. Plus, Anne's mother has lived with them for most of their marriage.

But they both agree that the last four years have been
better, particularly with Charles seeking help for his
drinking problem.

As is typical of her illness, Anne has accepted most of
the blame for the Fowlers' marital problems. She never
developed any self-confidence. She spent most of her life
caring for other people and taking the blame for all that
went wrong. She was not sure what it meant to be happy.
She thought recurring depression was about all there was
to life.

"I've never been manic," she said. "It's always depressive. I'd love to be manic."

Their first child, a daughter, was born a year after they
were married.  Anne had hoped a family would stabilize
the marriage and her depressions. But it didn't work that
way.

"My first child was a very difficult birth," she said. "'I
almost lost my life. I was in the hospital three or four
weeks. I had to come home in an ambulance.

"My husband was driving a cab then. There was no
telling where he was, and I never asked. I never felt like I
deserved an explanation. He stayed with me. I was determined that I was going to have a father for my children,
and they really adored him. I never felt worthy of him."

Another difficult birth produced a second daughter.
Then the Fowlers had a son, who was named for his
father. Anne said she her role in life was to be the best
mother she could possibly be.

"I had my children like they were never going to leave
me. They were mine, and I was always going to have
them."

It wasn't that simple, of course. When her son was
about 3 years old he was accidentally locked in a suitcase

for several hours. The suitcase had been left on the porch, he had climbed into it, and a handicapped boy who lived in the neighborhood had closed it. Anne said her son recovered, but he was slow to develop physically because he had became severely dehydrated and then developed emotional problems.

"I blamed myself for that," she said. "He had long-term mental complications. He would set fire to my clothes and let the air out of my tires, so we had to separate him from me for a while and put him in a special school.

"He tried to run away all the time. We had to put up a stockade fence to keep him in, but he'd still climb over it. But he's fine now. He's working in Arizona."

For about a year Anne saw the same psychiatric counselor who was working with her son, but she did not believe it had any lasting effect on her illness.

The Fowlers had two more children, a son and a daughter. They now range in ages from 29 to 44. The children are very close to their parents. They come by often to see them or to check on their invalid grandmother.

But while the children were growing up, the situation was far from idyllic. Anne had recurring bouts of depression and could be very irritable and withdrawn. Charles, who was operating his own tile and marble business, drank. He also began playing drums with bands and was often gone six nights a week.

As the children grew older, several of them began to show signs of being depressives or manic-depressives. The oldest children were restless and hard to manage. Like their mother, the Fowler daughters wanted to marry early and get out on their own.

In the early 1960s the Fowlers' second daughter rebelled. Barely a teen-ager, she began running away and hanging out with older boys. She said much of what she did was a reaction to her parent's lifestyle.

The daughter, now 40, was treated in a hospital for manic-depression. Her daughter — Anne's granddaughter — would also later require hospitalization for manic-depressive cycles.

Anne said her own problems, compounded by trying to control a rebellious child, led her to attempt suicide in the early 1960s.

"To tell you the truth, nobody knew it. I went and parked the car and took about 60 aspirins. Somebody found me laying there and took me to the hospital, and then they let me go. My family didn't even know about it."

Thirteen years ago she tried to kill herself again. While in a deep depression, she deliberately drove her car into a tree in the neighborhood.

"I had my baby daughter at home," she said. "She was about 16 or 17 and getting ready to be married. I took her car and ran into a tree. The car reared back up and the motor was in my lap. They had to get the 'jaws of life' to get me out.

"I've always had a death wish. Even when I was a young child, somewhere from 6 to 7, I would go out and climb a tree in a lightning storm and hope it would hit me. I ran out there real quick, and half the time my parents didn't know I was out there.

"I will say the incident with the car will be my last suicide attempt. I have entertained suicide thoughts, but I thought everybody did. I thought it was a way of life."

In between those thoughts Anne concentrated on her children. When she was busy with them she did not have time to worry about her problems or dwell on her depressions."

"I'm always there for somebody else. It was just like
First Communion for my little boy. Everybody went to
Communion, and I said, 'Somebody's got to stay home,'
so I couldn't go. But I didn't say anything. I kept it in. I
never left the house. My children were my life. I was busy
constantly."

Looking back, Anne's children say they can see that
their mother was rarely happy. But they learned to deal
with it. They learned to cope — or to get out.

The deepest and darkest depressions in Anne's life
occurred after her children had left home. Her husband
was still working — with some periods of unemployment
— and playing with bar bands at night. Instead of trying
to communicate, they seemed to find ways to ignore each
other, even punish each other with their silences.

At that time Anne's mother was still well enough to
cope for herself. Anne, alone with many of her thoughts,
sought solace where she had always found it; she retreated to the basement of their South Louisville home. She
would spend a large part of six years down there, once
not coming up for six months.

"Some of my children would come in and try to talk to
me," she said, "but I refused to talk. I couldn't talk. I'd lost
all sight of reality. I wasn't hungry. I had water down
there. It was dark. There was no television. I remember
the couch got wet, and I just sat on another couch. It
didn't bother me.

"The children knew I wasn't coming up. They would
bring food, and my mother would bring food and put it
on the steps.

"I would come up occasionally. I'd think about Mom
and make sure she had her medicine. But then I taught

her to do her own medicine."

Anne knows why she hid; she wanted to be in her own world. But she has never understood the full nature of her illness.

"Changes frighten me. I was comfortable in a way with my fears and my rejection. My inhibitions sabotaged every dream and hope I ever had in life. I was my own worst enemy, but I was comfortable with that. Do you understand that?

"When I was downstairs in the dungeon, I was happy down there. There were no decisions to make. There were no judgments to make. I was free to lie down all day. That's all I did. I think the worst part of depression is indifference.

"My children didn't understand it. They would just say Mom was on her high horse. Then one day I got so weak that one of the children had to take me to the doctor because my body was all run down. I was upstairs for a while, then I went back downstairs again."

Yet neither her children nor her husband insisted she see a psychiatrist.

"I think Charles was saying, 'If that's where the damn fool wants to be, let her stay,' " she said.

To some degree, Charles admits, he was saying that. He said he didn't understand his wife's illness. It's only been fairly recently that he has.

"I'd say up until about 10 years ago we didn't know anything about it," he said. "That's when I went to a self-help group and started worrying about my damn problems, and I kind of started focusing on her and taking her inventory. And she was taking my inventory. In other words, we started communicating."

But they were still a long way from solving their problems.

Charles said his wife started withdrawing from many things more than 10 years ago. He said he was a "river rat," he liked to get out, to be on the river, to meet their friends, but his wife stopped going. He said he did not drink heavily early in their marriage, but his jobs in the bars led to problems.

"It was the environment," he said. "It wasn't what I wanted to do. Everybody else was drinking. Everybody else was spitting on me, so I said, 'Hell, I might as well get into the act.' So I started drinking.

"I played music six nights a week. I had all the damn company, all the damn environment, all the damn partying. I had all the freedom I needed."

Charles said when his wife retreated to the basement in the early 1980s he would go two or three months without seeing her. The children would come to the house and bring food, but Anne often didn't want to see them.

For the family, the situation became normal. Anne had tried counseling and had attended support groups for her husband's drinking problems, but she hadn't felt they had helped. Her children cared for her, but she had rejected outside help, and they were busy with their own families and problems. Her husband, often lost in his world, couldn't help.

"I was dumber than she was about her problems," he said, "and my drinking more or less added to them. I was playing music, and I didn't care. I didn't have anybody to answer to.

"She just withdrew from everything. The kids came and tried to get her, to take her out somewhere, but she wouldn't go. Sometimes she would come out to cook dinner, but that was it."

For all that, Charles and Anne Fowler did not consider a divorce. Beneath all the pain and the problems they still needed each other.

"I know damn good and well I love her," Charles said. "I don't feel guilty at all about (her problems). Sometimes I think about it, but I don't let it bother me. That's in the past, and that's it. I can't do nothing about it. It's already done."

About five years ago Charles stopped drinking and stopped playing music in bars. He stopped because alcohol was about to kill him.

"I had to quit. I was down to about 130 pounds. I was drunk for about 17 days, and that was the last one. It liked to put me in the ground.

"A guy asked me if the Holy Spirit hit me. I said, 'Hell, no. That damn ambulance and its red, white and blue lights and stretcher is what scared me.' "

Charles joined a self-help group for alcoholics. "I do a lot of talking and I get up there and tell a few stories. I'm a group representative. I'm doing a workshop out at LaGrange Reformatory."

Anne said that for the last four years Charles has been "a perfect husband," although she worries that he may begin drinking again.

"I just knew I was the cause of his drinking," she said. "I had gone to a support group (for families of alcoholics), and I couldn't accept the help.

"I don't know why. Anger came into the picture. I thought the group was the stupidest thing I had ever heard of in my life.

"They said, 'Be detached but with love. If your husband's drunk, let him stay in the car.' Still he was my husband, and I always kind of stood by him."

"I did leave the house once and went out with my son. We went on a cruise. I stayed with my son for about three months, and that's when my husband got real bad and they put him in the hospital, so I came home. As far as therapy for me, my insurance didn't carry it, and I didn't want it."

Her therapy has mostly been self-help books. She began reading them after being encouraged by a family priest.

"He said I was an intelligent woman even if I didn't go to school," she said. "Get a dictionary if you don't know the words and let the dictionary be your bible.

"So I got every book I could find. It's called cognitive therapy. I read books like 'Who Am I,' 'Why Am I Afraid of You?' 'Why Am I Afraid to Tell You Who I Am.' 'I never go to bed at night that I don't read.' "

"See, I figured out now we are what we think. And we feel because of that. Then we act upon it. If you're not careful what you think or how you think, you're going to get into trouble. I'm not saying there's days you wake up and there's no reason at all for depression. I can feel the mood coming on, even here in the house.

"Charles has learned if I'm depressed he might say, 'You want your breakfast?' and then, 'Oh, oh, she's in one of those moods.' Or he may come up to me and say, 'You're the ugliest one thing I've ever seen in my life.' "
Why don't you do something about yourself?' And I say, 'Well, I don't think I'm all that ugly, and I'm not going to let you ruin my day.' So I'm learning that way. I'm learning to control my thoughts. Not to condemn you and not to listen to you condemn me.

"Charles is still the king. I can't interfere with Charles. I don't argue with him. I don't even know today if I love him. Being happy is hard work for me. Love is hard work as well."

More recently Anne's mother suffered a stroke and now needs constant medical attention. Taking care of her mother has helped keep Anne occupied, and her depressions have been much less frequent.

Anne also has serious medical problems of her own, including a weak heart and emphysema. She is taking medicine for those problems but nothing for her depressions.

Yet she often feels better than she has in a long time. She is learning how to reach out and touch people, something she's long been unable to do. But she is uncertain what might happen if her mother dies and she has no one else to whom she can devote her time.

"I'm better now because I have a job to do," she said. "Somebody needs me.

"There's some days I hate the trees and I hate the birds and I hate God. I don't know why the birds sing and I'm not. I know sometimes when I get up in the morning and I see the sun and I say, 'Oh God, you and your sun.'

"I try so hard to get in touch with God. I have tried it, but maybe I don't know how.

"Even when I'm not in a deep depression, my life is flat, boring, monotonous, stale and utterly wearisome without much hope or purpose. My goal in life is to someday feel it is a joy to be alive. What a fantastic journey that must be. I'm looking forward to that day."

Chapter Three

# GLORIA LIGHTSEY

*"I was just in pain,"
she said. "My whole
body was in pain. I
started to cry again,
but I couldn't get it
out. I couldn't get
the anger out.
"My anger had
imploded. That's
what depression is--
imploded anger. You
can't express it. You
implode it instead of
expressing it."*

For almost three years Gloria Lightsey has saved a one-page article from McCall's, an article she tore from the magazine after reading it in her sister's home while fearing she would never find anyone who understood her mental illness. It was a short, concise explanation of mood swings, and it may have helped saved her life.

"I think," she said, "I'm going to have it framed."

The frightening part was that Gloria had already been to several doctors seeking help for her manic-depressive cycles. She had fought the cycles for 15 years, helpless as they occurred more frequently. She had become unable to finish even the simplest tasks, or communicate with family and friends.

Teaching was the greatest joy of her life, but she became nearly numb to the children. She was filled with intense guilt because she could not find the answers even in her deep Christian faith. She began to harbor suicidal thoughts, and once tried to kill herself by running her car off the road.

Even then she was admitted to the maternity ward of her local hospital rather than the psychiatric ward.

As her illness became worse, Gloria's parents became concerned but did not know how to help. One family doctor said her problems were stress-related and prescribed rest. Another doctor prescribed large doses of vitamin pills. None could — or would — tell her she was manic-depressive.

Then, at age 26, having just been released from the psychiatric unit at the Duke University hospital — knowing she still hadn't found the answers — her sister showed her the McCall's "Monthly Help Newsletter," just one of the thousands of brief, simplified medical-advice articles that appear in supermarket magazines each year.

The article was about relatively mild "mood swings." It did not even specifically address her problems, but it was close.

"That was me," she said. "That was the first time I realized I was manic-depressive."

Gloria Lightsey's story is all too common with manic-depressives. Their disease is often misdiagnosed, often placed in the general medical ballpark with schizophrenia. Sometimes manic-depressives are given psychotherapy for years when the only permanent solution is to try to correct this brain disease with drugs such as lithium. In fact, there remains a lot of debate in the medical community about the diagnoses and treatment of manic-depressives.

For Gloria Lightsey, the answer came just in time.

"I was so upset with some of my doctors," she said. "The nurse of one of my doctors told my mother I was manic-depressive, but the doctor never told me. I knew I was sick, but I didn't know what it was."

Time, patience and lithium have solved many of Gloria's problems. She has faced her illness so squarely that now, as a student at the Southern Baptist Theological Seminary in Louisville, she is able to educate church groups and school classes about her illness. She taped an interview to be shown to other people. And she is back to doing what she loves best: teaching.

Lithium has not been the total answer. Gloria still needs anti-depressants for her occasional depressions, but she feels much better about herself — and her future.

"I was just thankful," she said, "that it all just worked out."

Gloria Lightsey was one of those children who, on the

surface, seemed an unlikely candidate for any kind of mental problem. While she was in school in Greenwood, S.C., her nickname was "Glo," a tribute from her friends who found her warm, bubbly and always eager to please.

The nickname seemed a perfect fit. Gloria had always been popular in school and involved with her church, although she was always a little reluctant to assert herself in peer-group situations. Her family had lived in or near Greenwood for generations, mostly involved with two of South Carolina's best-known industries: farming and textiles. Life seemed good and comfortable in the community of 40,000.

Only life wasn't always that good and comfortable for Gloria Lightsey. But her friends rarely saw her depressions.

"I'd go into my room and crawl into bed," she said. "Mother would notice because my room would look terrible, and I usually kept it pretty clean.

"Yeah, I'd go to school then. But I'd go to school sometimes with real puffy eyes. I'd been crying all the time."

Gloria was the third of three daughters in her family, with a gap of about six years between herself and her middle sister. She was intelligent, but school was not easy.

"When I started school in the first grade there were 40 kids in the class," she said. "Since I was the youngest child, I was the one who needed a lot of attention.

"I made B's and C's. I hated achievement tests. I quit taking one in the first grade. I just put my head down."

Gloria remembers a lot of details like that, details that come rushing back 20 years later, still carrying enough sting to hurt.

"Another thing I've learned from being a manic-depres-

sive is we have pretty good memories. I don't have a
good memory when it comes to grades, or things like his-
tory. But I have almost a photographic memory of some
things in my childhood, of things that have happened to
me. That can be painful at times, and it also can help me."

In retrospect she can see the many swings in her moods,
dating from the time she was a young girl. But she had no
label for them then. She thought the swings were normal.
There was no way to know the difference.

"I was a very sensitive child. I can remember when I
was 5 and I had said something or did something wrong.
We were getting ready to go get ice cream with another
family and something didn't set right, so my father made
me stay home.

"That really upset me. Dad never really let us express
how we felt. So I can remember laying in my bed, keeping
the door shut all night and not moving. I was 5 years old.
That may not have been a clinical depression, but I could
see the difference in my mood. I remember that vividly.
Very vividly."

Gloria was a pretty child but very late to develop physically. She had a fine, full singing voice, but her natural
voice was high and girlish. Her voice and thin frame were
physical attributes that often magnified her natural shy-
ness and insecurities.

"In junior high I was really skinny," she said. "That's
when I had asthma the worst. I guess I wore a size 3 or 4
dress. I had braces, the whole bit, and no form to me at
all.

"My psychiatrist told me later my manic-depression
could have slowed down my maturing process. I don't
know if that's true, but it made sense because the manic-
depression has so much to do with your emotions, and I

would be a really happy child or a really sad child."

In high school, the "Glo" was often what her classmates saw. She was in the student council, the glee club, played the guitar with a local church group  and was a good artist, at one time considering a career as an art teacher.

"We didn't date much," she said. "We just kind of went around as a group. I didn't start to develop physically until I was in the 12th grade. I was always behind everyone else. I was little. I was scrawny. I had asthma. I was always the type of child that would get hurt in friendships. I was so sensitive."

And she wasn't able to fight back. She could joke about her high-pitched voice and her skinny body, but the hurts could easily push her into depression.

"I was always nice," she said. "I never said anything bad, and even that was hard for me. If my friends would smoke or drink or whatever, I was always the one who didn't. I was the one who got the citizenship award, and I think I got an award from the glee club for being most congenial, or something like that. But all the time I still had my moments of depression."

In the middle of her recurring depressions, which would become more serious, Gloria had one marvelous "high" period in high school, a manic time she can recall fondly and just as vividly as her depressions.

"When I was in student council," she said, "I was chosen with another student to go to a high school student-council convention in Texas. There were 1,500 kids there from all over the United States. It was just wonderful.

"I had low self-esteem because of all the other things, but nobody in Texas knew that. So when I went to this convention they just pumped me up and made me feel like I was the best I could be. I was so high from meeting everybody and having the best time."

The group went to Six Flags Over Texas and had a dance at a big hotel in Dallas. She came home full of confidence.

"I couldn't sleep for about four nights. I was thinking about it all the time. I would talk 90 miles an hour and I couldn't stop. I really think a lot of my relatives and my friends now think back on that time and see it as a high."

Gloria had no more control over her highs than she did the lows. But the lows occurred more frequently.

Some of her problems were apparently hereditary. Although it wasn't discussed much in her family while she was growing up, Gloria eventually learned that she had a relative who had depression problems in college.

"She was very creative, very artistic," Gloria said. "She was a teacher and was very well-liked in her school. When I got real sick the first time and went into the hospital she was one of the first ones to call me."

Gloria also discovered that her grandmother had been so upset when her only daughter, Gloria's mother, married that she ended up in the hospital, where she received shock treatments. Gloria learned about all this when she herself was hospitalized.

"My grandmother was a very sensitive woman," Gloria said. "So sweet. I'm like her in a lot of ways."

She also learned that her father's parents suffered with depression. Her father was one of 10 children, five boys and five girls. Three of the boys fought in World War II and two of them were killed; Gloria's father survived.

Gloria said her parents did not show signs of depression. She said they were always very loving and very supportive but were not the kind of people who let their emotions show.

"They kept everything in the closet," she said. "They never showed their anger, so we didn't know how to express our anger. They never had an argument in front of us. If we got upset, we were wrong. My dad would say, 'Be quiet,' and they would never give us the chance to express ourselves because they were taught that it was bad to be angry."

As she moved closer to making a decision about where to go to college, the pressures began to build on Gloria, and her depressions became more frequent. About the time she received her award for being the most congenial in glee club, she would find herself crying uncontrollably with the group, even while singing.

"I had a really bad time in 12th grade," she said. "I had a difficult time trying to decide where to go to college. I knew I wanted to be a teacher, but I didn't know where I wanted to go to school. My dad said I could go anywhere I wanted, but I just couldn't decide."

Gloria said other factors added to the stress of her senior year. She was in charge of decorations for the prom, and once given an assignment she always felt a strong obligation to do it exactly right. She had also been elected minister of youth in her church, and she had to worry about delivering a sermon.

"I had a hard time dealing with those stressful situations," she said. "I can remember going to my room a lot and closing the door. When my friends would go out, I wouldn't go with them. I would start crying in class, and that was hard, especially when I was in glee club and singing. That's where it would really come out."

Her parents worried but thought her moods were probably due to stress.

Her friends were also concerned but didn't know

enough about mental illness to even begin to understand what was wrong. Gloria and her high school boyfriend broke up, mostly because of her depressions.

"My friends were all ready to go to college and here I was, I wasn't ready to go," she said. "But I knew that I had to go. I wanted to go to a college where I could become independent.

"I was very slow in everything that I did. When we would go get clothes for college I would start crying in the department store. It was just real intense."

Finally Gloria chose Appalachian State, a strongly Christian school in Boone, N.C. But the decision did not cure her anxiety or depression.

"My parents took me to college," she said. "When they took me I was crying all the way. Of course, my parents hid their emotions so they wouldn't upset me."

Gloria now understands that her parents were coping as best they knew how. No one had any idea how sick she had become. There was no one to advise them or help them.

"I was feeling a physical pain," she said. "It hurt. It really hurt."

Once enrolled at college, Gloria's depression became worse. She was confused and unable to cope. Her first roommate was also a depressive and abused alcohol. For the first time Gloria began to think about committing suicide, but she never really wanted to act on those thoughts. She moved in with another student, and her depression lifted a little.

"I found some friends. I think I got more adjusted. I think that's the word for it."

And the cloud lifted. She went home for Christmas in a very good mood; she had made new friends, had a B average in school, and the depression was gone.

Not that she knew what the problem had been.

"I didn't know the word 'depressed' explained what I had been feeling. I really didn't."

She finished her freshman year with a full head of steam, worked as a parks and recreation director that summer in her hometown and returned to Appalachian State for a good sophomore year. There were some problems; her depressions often seemed to coincide with premenstrual syndrome, but they weren't serious.

"I'd have my small ups and downs. I would always have a time when I was a recluse for a day or two, and then I'd come out of it."

After sophomore year a roommate at Appalachian State transferred to Baylor University, a strong Baptist school in Waco, Texas. Gloria took some classes at Baylor that summer, liked the school and decided to transfer there too.

The move sparked another high period in her life.

"My parents were very supportive. Within three days I got accepted, I found a roommate and an apartment. That was when I could see the highs coming in."

But not for long. She was soon too busy, and with the work came too much stress.

"I was a little sister at a fraternity, and I was teaching children's Sunday school. At the same time I was trying to study. When I'm so excited or so depressed it's hard to study. I did poorly in the first semester. My grades were terrible. I just could not concentrate. I was doing everything else."

Her second semester was worse. Continually depressed, she began eating too much; the weight gain only added to her depression. For the first time she went to a counselor, a chaplain at Baylor, looking for help.

"He just said I was having a difficult time adjusting to college life. It was just a one-time deal. It didn't help."

Many manic-depressives are in their late teens or early 20s before their illness becomes severe. Gloria could sense her problems becoming deeper. At her parents urging, she chose to finish college at home at Lander College in Greenwood. But she could not shake her guilt.

"Everything was negative. I felt guilty that I was depressed, or had gotten down. I was feeling guilty that I wasn't doing what God wanted me to do. It was always God-related; what is God's will for me? I couldn't find it."

At 21 she began dating a man about seven years older, a man who had problems of his own.

"I'm the type of person who loves to do things for other people," she said. "He would make me feel guilty about things, he would manipulate me, only I never saw that. He was into drugs, and I wanted to save him."

Gloria said their relationship lasted about eight months, a time, she said, when she needed attention as much as she gave it.

"When it came to men, I always had a low self-esteem. He gave me attention. He was lonely and he was working the night shift and was just really down. I was always the one who wanted to help."

When focused on other people, Gloria was able to forget her problems, to concentrate on her schoolwork. By the end of the school year at Lander she was student-teaching in a fourth-grade class.

"I even got on a high again. Sometimes I would stay up late at night, or I would have a night where I would just get the best creative ideas for lesson plans. I could go for a couple of days and never sleep at all."

Happy, and still somewhat attached to her boyfriend, Gloria at first refused an opportunity to student-teach in England. It was actually her boyfriend who pushed her into seizing the opportunity, even though it would separate them.

"I wanted to stay because I thought our relationship would end," she said. "He kept telling me, 'Gloria, you need to go.' So he was good in that way. He is a good person, deep down."

The separation gave Gloria some needed independence. She went on a "useful high," able to use her energy to her advantage without becoming manic. Many people with mild mood swings learn to do that, to call on the energy when it is needed but not to let it destroy them.

"My stay in England was one of the highlights of my whole life," she said. "I was afraid to go by myself, but I did it. We camped out for eight days with 75 kids. It was a blessing that I went to England at that time."

She finished college at Lander after the fall semester of 1983 and immediately began teaching seventh and eighth grade in a small school in the little town of Ninety Six just outside Greenwood. The former teacher had been much loved by the students, and Gloria was apprehensive about taking her place. She was also apprehensive about teaching in junior high, the same level where her mental problems had begun.

"The principal was very intimidating," she said. "He was a very loving man inside, a very dedicated Christian man. But he was the type of principal who, when you called in sick, would hang up on you. I was innocent and shy, and he scared me so much."

Gloria was living by herself in an apartment. She taught English and worked very hard to build up her confidence and to gain the respect of the students. She failed her teacher's licensing exam the first time but was allowed to continue teaching. Finally — with a lot of support from her principal — she passed the exam. She had lasted a semester as a teacher and felt very good about it.

"That summer I was determined to just have fun and go visit people," she said. "One of my cousins got married a week after school, and I was in her wedding. My cousin can remember me doing cartwheels and flips in the pool. I was talking 90 miles a minute and cracking jokes. I wrote a song for her that night and played it on my guitar while she was trying to get dressed for the wedding. That was a real high. When I went home I was exhausted for a day or two, but the rest of the summer I was fine."

She dated an old friend that summer but wasn't able to sustain the relationship. They never drew especially close or became intimate.

Then she met another man, the vice president of a small boat parts company from Seattle. Their relationship was very close and intense; for the first time she thought she had found the man she might marry. She had not considered launching a career first, then getting married and starting a family. Her goals were more traditional.

"I always thought I might get married after college. That's when my sisters got married. I'm kind of like the motherly type with kids, and that kind of thing."

But when school began again in Ninety Six, her new boyfriend quit calling and eventually returned to Seattle.

She couldn't figure out what had happened. Her depression returned with a vengeance.

"I knew something was wrong. I wanted him to say why he wasn't calling me, or just tell me what was wrong. But then I was chicken, and I couldn't communicate with him either. So I just tried to live without him."

She plunged into a depression that was aggravated by an enormous workload at school. She was teaching sixth and seventh graders in the same room but at different levels. She lost an excellent aide. She was assistant track coach, cheerleading sponsor for basketball and football and was tutoring a girl with leukemia, a quadriplegic, a girl who was pregnant and a student who had been in a car accident.

"Around October or November Daddy came to see me one day at my apartment," she said. "It was raining. I had six piles of clothes on the floor that I hadn't washed. I had maybe two weeks' worth of mail on the table that I hadn't even opened. I had glasses and dishes everywhere.

"Daddy said, 'Gloria, you need to come home. There's no way you can function here.' "

Gloria was 25 and still unable to seek professional help.

"When you're depressed it's hard to take the initiative. I didn't want to go to my church counselor because I didn't want anyone to see me. I was the one who was supposed to take care of everybody else. I was the one that smiled and was happy."

Her parents were not ready to take her to a psychiatrist, nor did Gloria want to go. Thinking the problem might be related to PMS, she went to her gynecologist. He prescribed some anti-depressants that rocketed her to a high.

"I went up. My kids loved it. We had the most creative lesson plans. I would just work day and night. I was just going 90 miles a minute, but I was having a great time and feeling good. I couldn't eat anything. I dropped about 12 pounds in a month."

At Christmas her old, manipulative, self-destructive boyfriend from her college days called. Against her better

judgment she spent some time with him. It was a disastrous visit, and she plunged back into a depression.

This was very early in January 1986. Withdrawn, rock-
ing back and forth on the floor at her parents' home, she
saw a television commercial about a man going through
depression. She looked at the TV and saw a mirror image
of her problems. She called her gynecologist and asked
what she should do. He said to take two anti-depressant
pills instead of one.

This time the medication had the opposite effect. She
felt as if she was in the bottom of a black pit, unable to
crawl out. Her entire body was burning. Totally losing
control she searched the house, found the car keys where
her parents had hidden them and went off to kill herself.

"I was worried about my principal and what he might
think of me. I was driving toward Ninety Six and, of
course, I was driving slowly because I was depressed. I
just decided I didn't want to feel like this anymore and
flipped the car on its side on the side of the road."

The car's slow speed — 35 to 40 miles an hour — and
the fact that she was wearing a seat belt, saved Gloria.
The car stopped on its side about 12 feet from a telephone
pole. Students from the school where she taught found
her.

"I was right across the street from a policeman's house,
so he came over," she said. "The police noticed my pupils
were dilated and asked if I had been drinking, or on
drugs. I said I was on medication, and I happened to have
the bottle with me.

"The policeman said, 'What do you do for a living?' and
I said, 'I teach school.' He said, 'No wonder.' So he drove
me home. He didn't charge me at all."

He took Gloria to an aunt's house where her parents

came to pick her up. Her parents knew about the wreck but didn't know it had been a suicide attempt. Gloria barely knew it herself.

At home, she spiraled into a complete mania. Her parents had gone to bed, but she stayed up all night, cleaning out all her drawers and her closet. She took two tests for graduate school in 50 minutes, tests that normally take 50 minutes each, and did very well on them. She found about 30 old Christmas cards, struck out the yuletide greeting and sent them to friends, writing "Happy New Year anyway."

Manic flights are often like that. To outsiders they can seem ludicrous, even humorous.

"About six o'clock in the morning I was swinging in my old swing set behind the house," she said. "Mom and Dad looked out the window and didn't know what was going on. I wasn't sure what was going on either, but by 7:30 I was vacuuming the whole house."

An old boyfriend from high school came by to take her to church. Her high continued. On normal Sundays people took turns reading Scripture. Gloria read all of it. Later she and her old boyfriend went to the country club; Gloria was aggressively friendly, greeting everyone, talking all the time, even to strangers.

But night she began to crash again. She called the hospital and was admitted — to the gynecology unit.

"I guess it's because my doctor lived in our neighborhood, or something. It's a small town, a small hospital, the whole bit. But I didn't know what was going on. They gave me sleeping pills. They gave me everything. But I couldn't sleep."

The next day, alternating between anxiety attacks and depression, she felt hopeless. Her mother came, saw her daughter, and cried. Then the staff psychiatrist came by, and Gloria told him she had attempted suicide just a day earlier.

"That was the first time I'd gotten professional help," she said. "And all the time I was worried about my students, about being a schoolteacher. I was wondering what my principal was going to say because he had always been so intimidating to me.

"So he called me up that day and he told me, 'I just wanted to say that I love you.' "

Gloria stayed in the hospital about a week and was discharged to go home and rest for a few weeks. The psychiatrist came to see her in the hospital on a regular basis and would continue to see her on an outpatient basis.

He led Gloria to believe that her problems had been caused by the breakup of her relationship with the man from Seattle. She said no one wanted to talk about any reaction to the dose of anti-depressants she had taken just prior to her suicide attempt.

"They were still not using clinical terms like manic-depressive with me. I now feel like he knew that's what I was, but he wouldn't tell me. Mom told me much later that the doctor's secretary had told her I was manic-depressive, but he wouldn't tell me.

"That's what I get angry about. Because I believe in communication, and I know it's difficult to say, 'You're manic-depressive,' but to hide that from me, and to hide the fact I had a drug reaction, it really made me mad. That would have helped relieve some of the guilt."

Gloria went home to recuperate before returning to teaching. She was given more medication for anxiety and depression, and bounced back to a mild high. She went back to school and had a great week, working 12 hours a day. But on Friday of her first week back, a day she was supposed to chaperon the school dance, she received a letter from her Seattle boyfriend ending their relationship forever.

"When I got to the dance that night I was so depressed my body was numb. I was totally out of it. Somebody took me home, and I couldn't stop crying."

She called her mother, and they walked around the block, nearly a mile.

"I was just in pain," she said. "My whole body was in pain. I started to cry again, but I couldn't get it out. I couldn't get the anger out.

"My anger had imploded. That's what depression is — imploded anger. You can't express it. You implode it instead of expressing it."

Still, Gloria went back to school on Monday. She couldn't function. She couldn't grade papers. She could barely talk.

"By Thursday I had the kids read the stories because I couldn't read. I sat there like a puppet with its strings down, and nobody had pulled them up yet.

"An aide pulled me from the room and took me to the teachers' lounge. I told her I just couldn't go on. The kids deserved better than that."

Gloria went home to bed for three days. She was given more anti-depressants, but they did not help. It was then that she experienced the worst moment of her life outside of the suicide attempt.

"I had an anxiety attack. It was the worst ever. I was just screaming, trying to get my anger out. It was a terrible scream, like EHHHHHHHHH, EHHHHH. My mother was the only one in the house, and I was just going crazy.

"My mother put me in the tub to try to calm me down,

and I was just screaming and pulling my hair. I can only imagine how my mother felt watching all that."

Her parents, worried sick, had Gloria see a doctor in Atlanta. After extensive testing he put her on a daily diet of 27 vitamin pills, allergy medicine and a little lithium.

Her mood swings continued as she puzzled over what to do about her professional life. She decided to attend the Southern Baptist Theological Seminary in Louisville to earn a master's degree in divinity with an emphasis on Christian education, which she later changed to counseling.

In March 1987 she visited Louisville to interview at the school, bringing all her pills with her. She was accepted. That May she sang at a wedding in South Carolina and found the experience very tense.

Her depressions and guilt had returned. Her new dose of medicine helped but did not end the cycles. She went to the Duke University medical school for more extensive mental and physical tests.

Her doctor at Duke offered Gloria some brief advice regarding her previous medication.

"He told me to get rid of all that crap."

She stayed at Duke for three weeks, moving from depression to a mild mania. Her doctor there never saw it; he was leaving for a job in another state.

The morning Gloria was discharged she fainted. She had been poked, prodded and analyzed but still didn't believe anyone had found the answers. Her parents picked her up at the hospital and took her to her sister's home in Virginia Beach, Va.

"When we left the hospital Mom and Dad knew something was wrong," Gloria said. "I couldn't talk. I was wringing my hands. I was very anxious."

Gloria wanted to stay with her sister, a former nurse. She was there about a week when her sister showed her the article in the June 1987 McCall's about mood swings.

"I couldn't believe it," she said. "It was about me."

She returned to Duke with the article. A doctor read it and with no more testing prescribed lithium. She began with 300 milligrams a day, was eventually boosted to 1,800 milligrams and now takes 1,500 milligrams. Her doses are above the average of 900 to 1,200 milligrams usually prescribed for manic-depressives.

That fall she came to Louisville and began school. She still has her mood swings, but they are much less pronounced.

"I feel like I'm in control most of the time. I do get a little high, but I've learned to use those highs creatively. I feel real good about myself."

Gloria believes it was the strong support of her family, her friends and her professors that helped her solve her problems.

"Being able to talk about it with everyone helped," she said.

She has a doctor in Louisville who counsels her. She still has her most difficult times during final exams or monthly PMS. But she has a lot more hope for the future. She expects to have her degree next spring.

Most important, she believes it has been her faith in God that has helped her survive and grow. She wants to pay Him back the best way she can.

"My emphasis will be in counseling, hopefully in a church or hospital setting," she said. "I want to help people through some of the problems I had."

*Chapter Four*

# JOHN MALUDA

*"When my son came home I was laying in bed saying, 'Hail Mary, full of grace, the Lord is with me.' I was just rambling it out. The psychologist at work later said I was in a panic and just stalling for time, more or less hoping that something would happen. If it wouldn't have happened, I was going to shoot myself."*

John and Rose Maluda

Rose Maluda remembers almost every detail of the moment she met her husband, John. It was shortly after the end of World War II, and they were both students at the Cincinnati Art Academy.

"I was about 19 and a freshman," she said. "I said I was going to my jewelry class. He said, 'Go get me a pair of pliers and some copper wire.' So I did. He said, 'Come back in an hour,' and when I did he had a complete necklace for me. He had it silver-plated. It was beautiful. I still have it. I still get compliments every time I wear it."

Rose soon learned that John Maluda was easily capable of such quick, brilliant displays of creativity. She found him exciting, attractive, intelligent and fun to be with.

They eventually married and began raising a family, two boys and two girls. But as John began displaying the symptoms of his manic-depressive illness more frequently, Rose often found it difficult to find the strengths that had so attracted her to him. As with many of the spouses of manic-depressives, the recurring cycles of her husband's illness could tax her strength as much as his, if not more so.

There were many times over the course of their marriage when she felt rejected, frustrated, angry and alone. She knew that John had little control over his problems; he was battling a serious illness that twice led him to attempt suicide and to be hospitalized several other times for manic or depressive episodes.

There were times when John was on a "high" that he would go on buying sprees that kept the family financially insecure. There were many times during his depressions when he ignored his family, wanting only to be alone.

There were also the times — when John acted more like the man she had married — when she was very happy in his company.

"I love this man," she said. "He's a wonderful man. He's got attributes all over the place. But he does not accept how people feel. That happens to be part of his background. There's nothing I can do about that.

"You get to a breaking point," she said, "and then he turns around and he is a nice guy again. So you have to weigh everything that's going on.

"People say, 'If you're so unhappy, why the hell don't you just leave?' It's just too involved. Are you going to leave just because he has an illness? Now what's that saying to other people who have an illness? What's that saying to your children, who might inherit it?

"The point I want to stress is that so much is being done now to treat the illness that people don't have to be afraid of it. It can be controlled. People don't have to suffer alone. They can and do lead good, useful lives if they will work at it and take their medication."

The Maludas have stayed together for more than 40 years, for "better or worse."

John worked very hard at his job at Standard Gravure all those years to support his family. Perhaps — and John always had to follow his union's dictates — he worked too long and too hard. He does not always see the things that Rose complains about, nor does he always agree with her perceptions of their life together.

"He has no recollection of things," said Rose. "It's like a drunk in a blackout. One of the things he does is put things in his subconscious so he doesn't have to remember it. He can stand there and tell you to go to hell and not remember it."

John believes his wife is a "very volatile woman" who
does not know what it is like to live with a mental illness
and the side effects of drugs such as lithium. He is a very
intelligent, very creative man who — especially in the
middle of a manic-depressive episode — truly does not
seem to understand his wife's frustrations.

Many manic-depressives do not; it's the nature of the
illness; it's what makes living with them all the more difficult.

"If I take any of that stuff she said seriously, it would
knock the hell out of me," John said.

Ever since he and a few high school friends made some
very ambitious home movies back in Clifton, N.J., John
has shown great flair for creating things with his hands
and mind.

He was one of five boys born into a family in which the
father insisted that all his sons quit school at 16 and go to
work. They were hard times, Depression times. John
stayed in school and earned his degree but also worked
in the family bakery beginning at 4 a.m. every day.

John also worked with his hands in art classes in high
school, especially sculpture. When his buddies proposed
the home movies, John photographed all of them. He and
his buddies were proud of the results.

"We were not the types that would go around and steal
hubcaps," he said. "We used to go to the Museum of Modern Art in New York and watch the old silent films."

After high school he worked as an apprentice to a sculptor in New York. He taught himself, reading a lot of
books on sculpting and going to night school.

"As an apprentice I carved wood and stone," he said. "I
got a lot of books out of the library. I was always one for
digging into the library. I was more or less a loner. If I

didn't know anything, I'd go and try to find someone to tell me about it."

With his arts background and the need to earn more money, John moved to Cincinnati in the early 1940s to work at a gravure plant and attend the Art Academy. He did well at the academy, putting on a few exhibitions and receiving small commissions for several jobs. But the money did not matter; he took the jobs for the experience and his own pride.

He had talent, but events in a troubled world conspired against him. On the day he learned he had won a $1,500 prize that would have enabled him to pursue sculpting almost full-time, he also received his World War II draft notice. The $1,500 prize went to someone else.

John was in the Air Force for 3 years, serving as an aerial photographer and gunner in Europe, tasks that required that he alternate between fighting off attacking planes and photographing the bomb drops. On the ground he used two sound cameras, fairly new in the military, and was part of the first Air Force unit to interview people on film.

John was able to do some sculpting work while overseas, but for the most part his art career was put on hold. When he returned to the Art Academy in Cincinnati after the war he learned that a rumor had circulated that he had been shot down and killed; much of the artwork he had created before the war had been thrown away accidentally.

He returned to the Cincinnati Art Academy determined to continue his career and becoming active in the arts community. It was during that time that he created one of his best works, a strong bronze figure he called "Vehement Moses." It was also during that time that he met

Vehement Moses

Rose.

"He was eight years older," said Rose. "He had been in the war. He had been all over, and I had been nowhere. I was living at the Anna Louise and eating peanut-butter-and-jelly sandwiches, and he asked me out.

"He was working as a photo engraver and going to school studying sculpture. It was just a slow accumulation of admiration."

The next year Rose, who was also intensely interested in art, wasn't able to return to the academy. She found a job in the art department at J.L. Hudson's department store in Detroit. They conducted their romance long distance and were married on June 25, 1948. Eight months later, when the Standard Gravure company in Louisville began to operate three shifts, the Maludas moved to Louisville so John could work here.

In their early years in Louisville John and Rose were busy and happy.

"We both went to art school in Louisville, and things were pretty good," she said. "We did have the normal ups and downs of marriage. We were very, very poor."

John worked briefly on the day shift at Standard Gravure, then worked the night shift for the next nine years as a color finisher. For four years he attended classes at the University of Louisville, studying sculpture under Romuald Kraus, his former teacher at the Cincinnati Art Academy. John eventually became a teacher at U of L.

"I went straight from work to U of L," he said. "I'd have breakfast at Masterson's and then walk across the street. I took sculpture, drawing, painting, crafts and some courses in medicine. After awhile Rose took some classes, and we would take classes together and go home together."

John also worked a lot of overtime at Standard Gravure, often seven days a week for months at a time, particularly during the holiday seasons.

"I was a young fellow then," he said, "and it didn't bother me to work the overtime."

The 1950s and early 1960s were a very focused, creative time for John. In 1953 he won first prize at the Kentucky State Fair in the metalworking division for a handsome silver teapot with a wooden handle.

A Courier-Journal article, which included a picture of the teapot, said John had developed "his own asymmetrical and yet beautifully balanced conical shape." It said John had also won prizes in the sculpture and jewelry competitions at the fair.

In December 1953 an article in the Courier-Journal praised him for his talents as a silversmith, featuring his silver pendants and sterling cuff links in an article about the Art Center's annual Christmas craft sale.

The article said: "John's wife, Rose Marie, also is a silver craftsman and has studied at the Art Center. But right now she is too busy raising a family to take any outside classes. They have two children, a son who will be 3 on Christmas Eve, and a daughter who'll be 1 on the same day.

"The Maludas have a plan to make most of the furnishings for their home. Right now John is working on a silver service and 'big hangings' in batik. His wife is making draperies and hooking rugs. (She has won state fair prizes for her rugs.)

" 'We hope to make all our hollowware, silverware, draperies and furniture,' he said. 'It may take a lifetime, but we'll have fun. We like original things.' "

The article also said: "John works as a silversmith at home as well as at the Art Center. When and if he has any spare time he likes to devote it to photography.

" 'Then every once in awhile,' John said, 'I find time to play tennis.' "

In 1955 John was featured in the paper again, this time for sculpting a 4-by-5-foot limestone bas-relief called "Mother and Child" for what was then the new Salvation Army Home on West Kentucky Street. He had spent several nights a week as well as week-ends carving the 3,000-pound block of white limestone.

Limestone relief entitled "Mother and Child," done for the Salvation Army Home on West Kentucky.

John, alone among the major contributors to the project, did the work for nothing. He did it to help the Salvation Army and to show the people of Louisville how exciting it could be to mix sculpture into building architecture.

"I was teaching sculpture at the time at U of L because Kraus was sick," he said. "So I took over for about a year, and the carving was my senior project. They told me to go ahead and give myself an A."

Three years later John sculpted a marvelous, 6-foot stat-

ue of St. Benedict for the Trappist monastery at Gethsemani, Ky. It took him 14 months to chisel it from another 3,000-pound block of limestone. His fee for that was $500.

"It wasn't much money," he said, "but I had never done it before, so I wanted to do it."

Staying busy during that period, John also crafted a huge cross for a Lutheran Church near Poplar Level Road, a cross for which he was paid $750 and spent

Sculpture done for Gethsemani

nearly $1,500 on materials. He was given another $500 to fashion church candelabras, spending $400 to make them.

He didn't worry about such things. He was an artist. He was staying busy. He just wanted to help others and create.

In 1955 the Maludas bought the house where they still live today. They had friends that were good, creative people. They went to parties. They enjoyed themselves. John knew there wasn't much money to made in his craft, at least at that time, but he could live with that.

"I saw how much trouble other sculptors had making it," he said. "At least I was putting food on the table. I wanted to be a sculptor all my life, but I couldn't make money on it, so I made my money from what I also knew I could do, photoengraving."

It was about 1960 when their fourth child, a daughter, was born, that John's family began noticing changes in him. He blames the changes primarily on job stress, the incredible amount of overtime he was expected to work at Standard Gravure while maintaining the quality of his work.

John began to feel more and more depressed. His wife saw the problems but tended to blame them on the eccentricities of a creative person. When he was depressed, his family learned to tiptoe around him.

"He used to be a very loving, very outgoing person," said Rose. "When I met him and before this illness he would help anybody. He would be the type of person you want to be around. You could count on him, and if he said he was going to be there, he would be there.

"Then he developed a certain quality where he would go so far, then back away. It was like he didn't want to get too close."

John had been a good father, a hard worker, a good provider. He began to drink more and spend more time with other artists. Rose said his moods would alternate. He became very compulsive, suddenly showing a great interest in guns. He became compulsively interested in fishing and outfitted the family with poles. Then he switched to bows and arrows and began buying them for his family. The entire house was soon stuffed with cameras, tape recorders, books and gadgets that John was constantly bringing home. Between the bouts of impulse buying, he would withdraw, not even speaking to his children.

"Then they built a big boat," Rose said, "and by the time he got finished making the boat he was so depressed he didn't want anything to do with it. It was like he would get exhausted with an idea and want to try something else."

John's mood swings had a profound effect on the family. Rose and the children, as is common in such house-
holds, thought they were doing something wrong. They
were no longer able to please him  and didn't know why.

"We were afraid to say anything because we didn't
know what kind of mood he would be in," said Rose. "We
went on vacation in Daytona Beach about 1962, and he
didn't have anything to do with the kids."

As John shut himself off from his family, Rose, the
daughter of an alcoholic, began drinking so she wouldn't
feel so alone; the bottle became her friend.

"After awhile I started drinking quite heavily," she said.
"I'd get my bottle and tell John to leave me alone, I didn't
want to talk.

"I really did like to talk and share things, but John
would have none of that. The mood swings after our last
daughter was born really became ups and downs. He
would smoke a lot, the smoke would lay and the depression would lay and you'd walk into this house and it
would be just horrible."

The Maluda children drifted away into their owns
worlds of ballet or art. They were tired of riding the emotional roller coaster between darkness and light.

"We begged him to quit his job and be a sculptor," said
Rose. "We would help him in any way we could. All the
kids loved him, and he was a good father. But we had
about 10 years of 'What did we do wrong, what's happening?'

John and his wife have different perceptions of that
period of their lives. John said his wife is very emotional,
and he doesn't know if some of the incidents were as
traumatic as she describes.

Nor can they agree on exact details of some incidents.

Rose is not as certain as John is that his illness is work-related.

"I don't know if what she says is true," said John. "That's the way she perceives things. That's not the way I perceive it."

But there was one undeniable truth: By the mid-1970s John was a very tired, very depressed man. He'd long stopped doing the major art projects he had so lovingly created 20 years earlier. He didn't complete many projects around the house. He'd walk out to the shop he built in his garage, look around and walk out.

"When you're sick, you don't do anything," he said. "You just try to make it from day to day.

"The depression came gradually. I just felt like I was dragging. I was not going to school anymore. All together 28 years of working that crazy overtime finally caught up with me.

"Sometimes we worked 60 days straight, sevens days a week. The only way you could get released from it was if you had a note from your doctor saying that you're sick. The union says that you can have time off if you have somebody to replace you, but if all three shifts are working overtime, who are you going to get to replace you?"

In about 1974 John went to a doctor for his depression and was given very small doses of Dexamil, which allowed him to continue to work. A year later the doctor switched him to Ritalin, a drug often given to hyperactive children. John became severely confused as a result of taking this drug.

He consulted a psychiatrist and was diagnosed as being severely depressed. He was given Thorazine. He researched the drug — as he has researched most things in his life — and began to fear that its side effects could

lead to heart problems. He remained depressed but
returned to work during the busy holiday season. On
Christmas Day 1975 he tried to kill himself with a drug
overdose, a mix of 55 pills.

"He was very depressed," Rose said. "Christmas was
very hard on him. He worked until 6 or 7 p.m. Christmas
night and went directly to bed.

"We had gotten into the habit of not waking him on
Christmas morning because he usually slept. About 3 or 4
in the afternoon a friend of his from work called and
asked if he was all right. He said he was worried because
John had been talking about 'the big sleep.' I said, 'Why
didn't you call me earlier' because he had just tried suicide."

John was in good enough shape that his family could
get him up and walk him around the house. He was taken
to a private psychiatric hospital by his son and his friend,
who had rushed over after the phone call. John was in the
hospital for two weeks.  Early in 1976 he returned to
work, never feeling he had received long-term help or
that his illness had been properly diagnosed.

"He was still being treated as clinical depressive with
suicidal tendencies," Rose said.

John's psychiatric counseling continued after the first
suicide attempt. He also learned he had a serious thyroid
deficiency that might have been contributing to his problems, and he was given medication for that.

In November 1976, the day before Thanksgiving, his son
found him at home in bed clutching a .22 rifle. John had
already fired one shot into the ceiling over his head to test
the weapon.

"We were working seven days a week," he said. "I was
doing retouching and had panicked at work. We had a

job that had to be done, that should have been done over. I said, 'It's going to take me two days to work on this.' The boss said, 'We can't do that. It has to be done by 4 this afternoon.' "

John said he thought he had really botched up the work. He went home, got the .22 and contemplated suicide.

"When my son came home I was laying in bed saying, 'Hail Mary, full of grace, the Lord is with me.' I was just rambling it out. The psychologist at work later said I was in a panic and just stalling for time, more or less hoping that something would happen. If it wouldn't have happened, I was going to shoot myself."

John estimates he waited 30 minutes for someone to find him. He was taken to his doctor, then admitted to the hospital where he had been treated after his first suicide attempt. He stayed there until near Christmas, was allowed to go home because a brother was visiting and was then transferred to another hospital where he stayed until March.

Rose insisted on the change in hospitals. She was frustrated with the first hospital because it was still treating John for clinical depression. She felt certain, judging from his actions at home, that he was a manic-depressive. It was a very difficult time for her because she had also begun working away from the house, was trying to take care of the children who were at home and was visiting with John two days a week, and making two other trips to speak with his social workers.

"I kept telling them any man who acts like John has to be manic-depressive," she said.

John saw a battery of doctors, including a psychiatrist, a psychologist and a psychotherapist. He was given a very selective, slow-acting anti-depressant that pushed him out of his depression right into another problem.

"I went sky-high," he said, "I began making long-distance telephone calls to my brother and everything else."

Rose saw the high coming even before the doctors.

"I went to see him, and John was pacing up and down. I knew he was on a high and out of control. When I get home, the phone rings. It's John. He's so high he told me, 'Pack your suitcase, we're going to Washington. I'm going to be Carter's aide, and you're going to be my common sense.' Then he slammed the phone down."

John said he was given another drug to help bring him down, a drug that made him so violently ill he felt he might die.

"It made me sicker than a dog," he said. "I had to walk and walk and walk to work it off. I told the doctor that stuff is supposed to cure me, not kill me."

When John's doctor's realized just how high the antidepressant had pushed him, his diagnoses was changed from depressive to manic-depressive. John was taken off all drugs for about a week to clear out his system and was then started on lithium.

"That was the first time I had heard of lithium," he said. "I took a blood test every eight days until I could get to the therapeutic level I required."

Finding the right level is always tricky and rarely permanent; many manic-depressives' needs shift constantly. In addition to his medicine, John was given group therapy, physical therapy and time to work in a craft shop.

He returned to work when he was released in March 1977 but under doctors' orders that he could not work more than seven hours a day five days a week. The extreme job pressure was off, but his income was also cut about in half. Rose kept her job, which helped, but the

Maludas would now have to cope with financial pressures as well as John's illness.

John took early retirement in 1982, at age 62. The lithium and the reduced workload helped, but his chemical needs kept shifting, and he was hospitalized several more times in the 1980s for manic-depressive episodes.

Right after his retirement he abandon sculpting and threw himself — with disastrous financial results for the family — into making a scaled-down musical instrument for children, a Montessori harp.

John had been working on the concept and a few small harps for years. The idea was to build an instrument about 1/4 the size of a real harp so children 3 to 6 years old could play it. He followed that idea with a Montessori psaltery, a flat, boxlike musical instrument with strings that very small children could play.

Often working on a high, John spent about $10,000 in two years developing the instruments, including thousands of dollars on recording equipment to make sales tapes. He bought books about Dr. Maria Montessori, the woman who developed techniques for teaching young children. He began writing a book about her and her teaching methods and having the photographs for the book enlarged. He called Ireland about her. He hired a secretarial service to do his typing.

"There was a period of about three years where Marie Montessori was a god," said Rose. "The amount of money was incredible. And every time he was high he would do things over and over and over again, just like a drunk.

"One morning he was up at 5 a.m. calling Ireland, and he hasn't got time for his family. He retired at 62 and in one year he went though all his retirement money."

Rose, like John, believes the scaled-down instruments

are a great idea. Other people think so to; at one point
John received a grant from the Bingham Foundation to
build 25 harps and 25 psalteries for Berea College, but the
project fell through because of personnel changes at the
school. Then John was hospitalized for depression and
had to reject the grant. He sold some plans for the instruments, but due to a lack of consistent marketing has made
very little money.

Rose believes the eight years since John retired have
been more difficult than the years while he was working.
She said this is partly because he does not always take his
medicine and his moods continue to swing.

"When he's up and manic he's moving all the time. He
goes two or three nights at a time where maybe he'll get
two hours' sleep a night. When he's high he goes, goes,
goes. He doesn't care about you or anybody else's
feelings. In depression he sleeps. He's uncommunicative."

One such episode is still vivid in Rose's mind. She had
returned home after a trip to Chicago, and John was obvi-
ously on a high. The moment has almost comic overtones.

"I stopped to get him some food," she said. "He had
decided he was going to put in a built-in stove. I come
home and the screen door is off and leaning against the
house. The door is open and it's summertime. The television is going full blast. The water's boiling on the stove.
He had bought a stove and you could not inch your way
past it.

"He bought a fan. He had taken the whole cabinet apart
and it was down on the floor. There were books in boxes
all over the place. He's laying down in bed with his hat
on, his boots on, his coat on, his headphone playing
music. I just turned off the water and left it."

As a result, there are now times when Rose counts the
number of pills left in her husband's medicine bottle to be
sure he is taking his doses, two 450-milligrams pills of
lithium every day. John resents that, accusing her of being
"nosy."

He admits there are times he does not take his medicine
because of its side effects; he has been taking lithium for
14 years and it's taken a toll on his body while helping his
mind.

"Lithium affects my gastrointestinal tract," he said.
"There are times when I don't take it because I want to
calm down my insides. When I get off it I take Prozac or
an anti-depressant until my stomach quiets down."

There are problems there too. Prozac, a controversial
drug, also causes John some stomach ailments. So there
are periods when he takes no medicine at all, but he does
not believe it greatly affects his mental condition. Rose
does.

"The reason I really wanted to do this book," she said,
"is to say the illness is not something to be afraid of if the
patient will work with the people involved in it, but I get
so frustrated when he will not take his medicine.

"There is a pattern to this. My belief with all my heart is
that when John is high I could drop dead right in front of
him, and he'd step over me. But when he's depressed he
needs me.

"It's called co-dependency. You put all your energies
into this person because you don't have an identity. You
lose your reality in them because they are such strong
individuals."

Rose stopped drinking eight years ago, joining a 12-step
program she said saved her life and taught her to step
back and look at the situation.

"If I went out again and started drinking myself to death, I wouldn't expect John to stay with me. So he has to understand that he has to take his medicine and do his part. If one thing doesn't work, you have to try another. There are new avenues opening all the time.

"He's better at communicating than he was, but to a certain extent he still shuts me out."

John has attended some of the family counseling sessions but not many. Rose worked part-time as a seamstress for local theaters, but recently retired from her job to collect Social Security. All their savings are gone. The Maludas live on pensions and Social Security, enough to get them by if John can curb his spending sprees. He is still prone to spending weeks shopping for cars the family cannot afford.

John is still battling his cycles, as he probably will for the rest of his life. In the late 1980s he went through a nearly two-year depression. When he is well he travels, and he and Rose have a good time.

"He often plays games," she said. "He's not always honest with me. But when he is well he's delightful, really delightful."

But as recently as last year Rose came home to find that he had fired a .22 shot into the window, a shot John said accidentally occurred while he was cleaning the gun.

John Maluda said he has one more big project he would like to try as sort of an exclamation point to his art career, a 12-foot bronze figure of Moses that would cost perhaps $12,000. He has sketches and models but nothing beyond that. If done, he said, it would be an "extra bonus" for his life.

If it doesn't develop, he said he wouldn't be too disappointed.

"Why should I be disappointed?" he said. "I earned my living. I made it to 62 to retire. I've learned to live with what I have the best I can. For some people that might not be so much, but it's the best I've got.

"You can't go running to the doctor and running to the hospital the first time you're getting depressed. You don't have the money to afford it. You have to work it out your own way."

*Chapter Five*

# FRANK MARX

*"My mother loved me very dearly and I loved my mother, but because of her illness I never experienced the closeness of a mother-son relationship with her. And then some years later I found out that I had a similar illness."*

Joanne and
Frank Marx

The best thing Frank Marx had going for him was that he could sell. He could sell clothing. He could sell chemicals. When he was aggressive and persistent — which wasn't always the case — he made a good living for himself and his family.

The problem was the time Frank Marx became so aggressive he almost sold himself into a $4.5 million disaster.

Incidents of terrible financial judgment are common among manic-depressives — especially people in manic phases. They find themselves in a state so high, with personalities so strong and minds so active that they believe they can do anything.

The danger is they almost can.

Well-connected businessmen quickly put together multimillion-dollar deals, or multimillion-dollar disasters. They become so focused, so full of themselves, so energetic that they quickly wear out subordinates and their families. But they have no real sense of the damage they are causing.

People on highs will go on shopping sprees, spending thousands of dollars on clothes, appliances or furniture they don't need, then crash into depression when the bills come due.

They can be "the life of the party," dominating any room with their antics and quick wit. They can start a dozen great projects and never follow through on any of them.

Some seek dozens of social relationships or pursue sexual conquests in a maddening frenzy. Manics become "super-organizers," easily able to handle two or three events at the same time. They cannot sleep, sometimes getting their employees or friends out of bed at 3 or 4 in the morning, throwing a half-dozen ideas at them — later forgetting they ever made such calls.

Frank Marx became so focused as a chemicals salesman that he was often able to make his quotas before noon. Then he spent the rest of the day at the racetrack. For many years he was heavily involved with horses and the people around them. It was a lifestyle he liked but couldn't really afford, even when he was making $50,000 a year.

He and his wife attended the Kentucky Derby every year. But one year, on a "high" and eager to prove that he belonged with the big hitters of racing, he borrowed $3,500 from a bank for box seats to the Kentucky Oaks and the Kentucky Derby. The bank gave him the money without question. The seats had a face value of $600.

He couldn't see what his illness was doing to him. He was so sick he once tried to persuade a psychiatrist that it was his wife who was mentally ill, not him — and he succeeded.

He was the best salesman in the Kentucky area for the Texas chemical company for which he worked, but he was fired because he was so contemptuous of his superiors.

So Frank and his wife, Joanne, started their own chemical sales company. It was successful, but Frank nearly threw it all away trying to buy a $4.5 million warehouse/office complex, a spur-of-the-moment purchase that probably would have forced him into bankruptcy. It fell through only when his wife, who owned 51 percent of their company, refused to sign the agreement.

Two days later Joanne signed a mental-inquest warrant and had her husband committed.

Frank Marx's race to get into the fast lane ended in a

mental hospital.

He had no control over his illness. It prevented him from thinking about his two sons — the pride of his life — who were attending very good, very expensive colleges. It could have destroyed everything he built, and considering where he started, he had built quite a bit.

"I was this close to making that deal," Frank said. "If it hadn't been for Joanne, I would have."

Frank and Joanne Marx recovered from that moment to form the Manic Depressive and Depressive Association of Louisville Inc. It's a self-help group for depressives, manic-depressives and their families. In five years it has grown from just a handful of people to almost 250.

Frank's willingness to acknowledge his illness, then work to overcome it and help others, has made him something of a role model to his sons. Their relationship remains solid and strong. Frank has proved that with enough love, understanding and family support, manic-depressives can function — and prosper.

His goal now is to raise $7.5 million to build a halfway house to help people like himself. It would be a halfway point between a mental hospital and home.

"I know what I've been through," he said, "and I know a halfway house could do wonders for a lot of other people."

As with many manic-depressives, Frank's serious mood swings — and he has mostly been manic — didn't begin until he was well into his 20s. But the foundation may have been laid with a difficult childhood.

"In my early life I was shifted around," he said. "I lived with different members of my family, and I was very bitter and angry. The thing that kept me alive and going was my anger."

His father died when Frank was 9. He had been a salesman, the same kind of driven, persistent salesman Frank would become.

"My father was really good. He was hard of hearing, and they didn't have hearing aids in those days, so he used to pick me up when I was in the first, second and third grade and take me down to where he was selling automobiles.

"He would pull me over to the corner and ask me what the customer said to him. I'd tell him and he'd go back and start selling again. He didn't want them to know he couldn't hear."

His father also spent a lot of late nights playing gin rummy in bars with his buddies. He didn't drink alcohol, only soft drinks, but he drank them endlessly.

"I think he died because of soft drinks," Frank said. "He drank six or eight every day. One thing that really frightened me and my mother was he went for a physical examination a year before he died, and the doctor told him if he kept eating those ham sandwiches and drinking soft drinks, he would be dead in a year. The doctor told him he could get better.

"So we left there and went to a place where we often ate lunch. He ate three ham sandwiches and had six soft drinks. When he did that, I just said to myself, 'My father's going to die.' I knew in my heart my father was going to die."

A year later Frank was taken to Jewish Hospital to see his father, who was very sick with uremic poisoning.

"My father was from a family of 13, and my mother from a family of 12," he said. "All my father's brothers were in the hospital room. They knew he was dying. He said he wanted to see me alone.

"Here was my Dad with uremic poisoning. He could hardly move, but he managed to get to the side of the bed. By that time, the urine scent was pouring out from all over his body. His shirt was soaking wet, and he stared at me straight in the eyes.

"He said, 'Son, I want you to do me a favor. I want you to always take care of your mother and your sister. That's all I wanted to tell you.' "

Frank Marx's father died the next day.

Frank's mother took the death very hard. Shortly after her husband died she had a nervous breakdown. She would be in a mental hospital for almost 12 years.

Young Frank went to live with an aunt, who was Jewish, as his father had been. His mother was Catholic.

"Aunt Rena raised me as a Catholic - all the way," he said. "She kept me stable. She expected me to be in by 10:30 or 11 every night."

Frank graduated from St. Xavier High School in 1950. He was an excellent tennis player. He'd worked hard at his studies the first two years, then coasted until graduation.

After graduation, Frank worked for one year at a wholesale clothing store as a stock clerk. When he received a draft notice from the Army early in the Korean War, he decided he would enlist in the Air Force instead. He was stationed at Travis Air Force Base in California. In the 12 years since his father had died he'd only seen his mother once; he came home on leave and visited her in a public mental hospital in Louisville.

"She knew who I was," he said, "but she had been in the hospital so long that she was more coherent with the ways of the hospital than she was with me. She hugged me, but I knew she barely recognized me because the last

time she had seen me I was just a little boy. That experience really had an impact on me. At that moment I knew
that someday I would do something about mental
health."

Frank's highs began to manifest themselves while he
was in the service, although he didn't recognize it. In two
years he went from private to staff sergeant, in charge of
sending other men on the base through technical school.
He was aggressive, sometimes loud and often opinionat-
ed, especially about his superiors. Yet he got along well
with the other men, did his job and succeeded.

"I was stable during most of that time," he said.

While Frank was in the service, an uncle had taken his
mother from the public hospital to his home to live.

But after living with her brother for a short time
Frank's mother became very hostile. She was given one of
the first lobotomies performed in Kentucky, which
improved her condition.  In fact, she was even able to
work. She moved in with her daughter about a year
before Frank got out of the service. He sent allotment
checks home to help pay the bills.

When Frank got out of the service in 1955 he joined
them. His sister married a few years later, leaving him to
care for his mother.

"Living with my mother was an unnatural thing," he
said. "I didn't want that. I didn't want to do it, but I felt
the loyalty. My dad had asked me to take care of my
mother. That stuck with me all my life."

Few people in his family had a college education. He'd
often been told he would never receive a college degree
because his father had only a sixth-grade education. That
pushed Frank to succeed, working with a fury that at
times seemed manic to other people. He got an under-

graduate degree from the University of Louisville in four years while working full time.

"I had a scholarship for tennis," he said, "I got money from the Veterans Administration because I had been in the service, and I worked eight hours a night at the post office to help support my mom.

"In class I would copy all the material the professors put on the board. Two days before the exam I would read all of the assigned material as well as what I had copied off the board. Then I would make a choice in my mind what to remember. That's what got me through.

"I don't know if I was high then or not. I had to work. I had to take care of my mother. I would eat, sleep, work, play tennis, and I also belonged to a fraternity.

"In manic-depression the illness manifests itself when you don't get sleep. I was so tired that when I got off work I would be dead asleep for six hours, and that made it normal. On weekends I would get some rest or do the things I liked to do.

"As long as you do what you like to do and aren't forced into a stressful position you don't have mood swings too often."

By the late 1950s Frank had became an assistant manager of a chain-owned clothing store. He was an excellent, aggressive worker but soon developed a problem that would follow him for years: He was always getting angry with management.

"My district manager told me if I had a better disposition I could run about eight or 10 stores," he said, "but I had a terrible disposition. I'd get angry. I'd get angry very quickly. Due to that I was never promoted."

In 1961 he went to work for Dupont in Louisville. In the spring of 1962 he met his future wife, Joanne, at a dance.

They were married on Feb. 9, 1963. Frank was taking some medicine for his nerves, but Joanne never saw the problems that were to surface in the next 25 years.

"I just saw Frank as a real up person," she said. "Very energetic. Even today you don't see him in the typical down position of a manic-depressive, those times when he becomes non-functional. Unlike the majority of manic-depressives, Frank experiences down periods when he is angry, not depressed."

Early in their marriage Frank's mother had her own apartment. During the week she lived with a sick girl for whom she cared; on the weekends she would live with Frank and Joanne.

His mother's temper would occasionally flare, which made everyone uncomfortable, but the family relationship survived. In time his mother had a stroke and was placed in a nursing home where she still lives.

And Frank is still taking care of her:

"My mother loved me very dearly and I loved my mother, but because of her illness I never experienced the closeness of a mother-son relationship with her. And then some years later I found out that I had a similiar illness."

Joanne began noticing symptoms of the illness about 1964. Frank would become very angry about things that didn't seem to warrant it, flying off in rages that could last a long time.

"I remember the first Christmas after Frank III was born," she said. "He was about 11 months old and he was very ill. We couldn't go over to our families' houses Christmas Day so my family suggested that they bring over a plate for each of us.

"Wow! Frank just blew a gasket. The very idea that my family would bring over some food. I don't remember what we did, but they didn't bring any food over.

"I tended to back down then. I didn't want to promote a lot of anger."

But the first incident that really concerned Joanne occurred in 1965. Frank had just switched jobs — going into sales for a chemical company — a switch that sent him to bed for a week in a deep depression.

He had gone to Chicago for the job interview but was told he wasn't going to be hired. As a parting shot, Frank told the interviewer that he was making a big mistake. The man followed Frank out into the hall and hired him.

"He just gambled on me," Frank said. "He didn't think I could make it. I got home and started thinking I was going to be working only on a commission. I thought, 'God, I bet I can't make it.'

"I got really scared and depressed. Every day it got worse. The thing that got me out of it was when I called my boss in Chicago and told him I didn't sell anything that week. He listened to me, and he said, 'Dammit Frank, get out of that bed and get to work.'

"It scared me, so I told Joanne I'd go up to West Virginia and work really hard. By the end of the next week I'd written $5,000 worth of business. One thing I'll never forget. Before I went to West Virginia the fear in me had been so great I couldn't even get out of bed."

Following that week's depression, Frank began seeing a psychiatrist for the first time.

"He told me I was all right. He told me to just get up and go to work and that there was nothing wrong with me."

The psychiatrist also suggested the Marxes have another child, so they did: a son they named Joe.

"We did what we were told," explained Joanne, laughing a little. "At that time in my life doctors were gods."

By the late 1960s Joanne saw another trait in Frank that bothered her; he would meet his quotas but wouldn't try to earn more. It seemed to her that he could have doubled or tripled his salary if he would work full days, but he didn't. He got involved in other things — such as politics.

In 1969 Frank ran for state representative. He was on a long high. He purchased $3,000 worth of stationary, bumper stickers and campaign materials. He couldn't sleep. He made early morning phone calls. He was trying to take care of his business and run for office. The stress was tearing him up.

He had begun taking Thorazine pills — depressants — like peppermint candies. Joanne reached her limit when she found Frank on the phone at 5 a.m. giving "holy hell" to one of her friends.

"I jumped out of bed and said, 'By God, I've had it.' Something is wrong. I've got two little kids to take care of. We're going to see a doctor."

She and Frank went to see the psychiatrist who had been treating his mother. While there, Frank convinced the doctor that it was Joanne — not him — who was sick.

"I was just trying to get across to the doctor all the things that had been going on," Joanne said, "and Frank was standing there saying, 'By God, this woman is nuts.' The doctor said I was having an anxiety reaction. He said, 'You two need to be separated. I suggest you go to the hospital.' "

Joanne was flabbergasted. She knew Frank was sick. But she believed in doctors, and she was so rattled by Frank's behavior that she began thinking that perhaps something was wrong with her. Her home life had exhausted her.

She went home thinking she was ill and did need to go to the hospital.

"We saw the psychiatrist on Saturday morning," she said. "I went home, packed a suitcase and got everything ready for the kids because I wasn't going to be there. Sunday night I was almost ready to go, and Frank broke down and started crying.

"He said, 'It's not you, it's me.' "

So Joanne took Frank to the mental hospital.

"I knew I couldn't take care of those kids," Frank said. "I told the hospital staff it was me, not her."

Frank was in the hospital for 30 days in 1969. He was given Thorazine and a series of eight electro-shock treatments to calm him down but was never diagnosed as a manic-depressive. He did not participate often in the normal hospital routine of exercise and group or individual therapy. He just let the medicine bring him down to a functional level, then he went home.

"My doctor said he didn't think he could help me anymore," Frank said. "He might have thought I was manic-depressive because he wanted to give me lithium, but he said my liver level was too high, and he was afraid. Then I went to another doctor that didn't believe in much medicine."

Lithium was a new drug in the United States in 1969, and its use was not widespread. So Frank found a way to doctor himself, to keep his life in balance.  For the next 14 years he would work sales in the morning, then go to the racetracks in the afternoon.

"I only took $30 a day," he said. "I didn't care if I won or lost. I used to lose about $250 a week."

As the horses moved from track to track, Frank made the circuit from Louisville to Lexington to Northern Kentucky.

"I would walk," he said. "I would walk from the grandstands to the clubhouse and make a bet. I'd talk a few
minutes, go back to the grandstands and back to the clubhouse. When I'd go home after that, I'd be so exhausted
I'd eat supper and go right to bed. I did that almost every
night."

There were exceptions to his routine. Frank remained
devoted to his children. He helped organize a tennis
league in which a son played. He would travel to watch
his son debate. He did everything for his children, but he
and Joanne didn't do much outside the home.

"I didn't like to be entertained, or to entertain," he said,
"unless it was a business deal that I had to go to."

Frank had plans beyond being a $5 bettor. He tried to
get involved selling tack and horse supplies to the group
that trained Spectacular Bid.

Operating in a manic state, Frank befriended Bud
Delp, the trainer of Spectacular Bid, and the groom and
exercise rider associated with the horse. He began getting
up at 4 every morning, buying a dozen doughnuts and
taking them to Keeneland where Spectacular Bid was sta-
bled.

"Every morning," he said, "Spectacular Bid would eat
two of the doughnuts and I'd throw the rest away."

Spectacular Bid won the Bluegrass Stakes and came to
Churchill Downs for the Kentucky Derby. Frank continued to buy the doughnuts. Spectacular Bid won the
Derby. Frank flew to Baltimore, home of the Preakness,
trying to sign a deal to market Spectacular Bid memora-
bilia. That deal fell through because all rights to Spectacular Bid's name had been given to the Opera Association
of Baltimore by the horse's owners. So Frank came home.

"But that was a high," he said. "That was a straight high."

Frank then turned to another venture. He and an old friend got involved selling handcrafted marble desk sets and whiskey bottles. They made a handcrafted whiskey bottle which was given to President Carter when he visited Bardstown, Ky.

Frank met Morley Safer of "60 Minutes" at the Kentucky Derby one year and was able to speak with him briefly, showing him pictures of the items their company handled. Later Safer's secretary called from New York asking about the items and Frank - on the spur of the moment - flew to New York to present a desk set to Safer, hoping it would help their business.

"My friend was the only person in the United States doing this type of work," Frank said. "I could never get the company off the ground. It was a bitter disappointment to me."

If Frank won money at the track — maybe $60 or $70 — he always brought it home to Joanne. But he never won big, and usually he lost.

"I was making good money," he said. "I was making $50,000 a year, but Joanne had $20,000 to live on, maybe $25,000."

Joanne was not happy with her husband's lifestyle, but she had the children to raise. She also began working part-time as a registered nurse. When the boys reached school age she began to work full time.

"I didn't realize Frank was going to the track every day," she said. "Maybe I would find the tickets in the clothes when I took them to the cleaners, or something like that.

"When I look back on it now it's hard to explain why I accepted it, but I was busy with the kids, I had a sick mother and I was busy working. I got real involved with my children when I wasn't working.

"The only thing that I can remember that stands out in my mind is that when he would come in every day I could almost tell the way he closed the door whether he had a good day or a bad day.

"I never knew what kind of mood he would be in, but it was never the exaggerated form that it had been in the past. He was just angry, and he would be angry at his customers, so I was glad when he went to bed."

Frank was going to see a psychiatrist every few months for his highs. He was taking the drug Atarax, but there was never a permanent answer.

"The psychiatrist would always say, 'Frank, your trouble is that you get at the top of the ladder and you always go down.' He said someday I would go over the top and my problems wouldn't be as bad."

But Frank never quite got to the top. In 1981 his employer fired him for his belligerence. He received $30,000 in severance pay, which is what he and Joanne used to start their own chemical sales business. At the time one son was attending Stanford, the other Notre Dame. The tuition costs were about $30,000 a year.

Frank had to work very hard, and he did.

"The boys always did very well in school," he said. "I always told them as long as they did well in school I would take care of the expenses. I really lived not only for my wife, but my two boys. They're the jewels of my life. I think I got that way from my father.

"Joanne always said they should go to a small college here in Louisville. I kept saying, 'Let them go to a big school,' so they would be satisfied with nothing but the best. That's the way they had their minds set, and I think I had a lot to do with that."

Frank III would go on to get a degree in mathematical
and computational sciences in four years at Stanford, and
receive his master's in engineering economic systems
from Stanford.

Joe received his undergraduate degree in government
and international studies at Notre Dame, earning Phi Beta
Kappa honors. He went on to receive a master's in international economics and international relations from the
Paul H. Nitze School of Advanced International Studies at
Johns Hopkins University. Joe is also a writer, having
recently authored a chapter in a book on international ter-
rorism.

The responsibility of paying for college expenses was
good for Frank. Whereas the pressure he put on himself
to run for state office had led to his first hospitalization,
he felt the pressure to work for his sons was beneficial.

"I really had to produce," he said. "Otherwise I would
have failed my sons."

Frank produced until 1985. Then another kind of stress
came into his life. He developed cancer on the outside of
his bladder.

"I was scared to death," he said. "I thought I was going
to die."

An operation and once-a-week chemotherapy got rid of
the cancer. But Frank did not calm down. He continued to
take Atarax like candy. He believes the drug may have
induced an even higher manic state. He had delusions; he
came to believe he was the Holy Spirit and that Joanne
was the Blessed Mother.

"There was a very gradual elevation of his mood after
the operation," Joanne said, "but I knew he wasn't sleeping and that something was going on. I thought when the

chemotherapy was over he would get better. But I knew
he was in trouble, very serious trouble."

Frank's problems came to a head in óne bizarre, frightening five-day period in 1985.

Despite his obvious mental problems, he insisted on
working. The business, in fact, was doing fine. Thinking
of future growth, Frank put on a $300 suit one Wednes-
day morning and went looking to lease a warehouse-
office complex Joanne had heard about.

The real-estate agent proposed to Frank that instead of
leasing it he buy it for $4.5 million. The agent knew Frank
didn't have that kind of money but suggested that the
owners of small businesses in the complex, unhappy with
its current management, might put up money as collater-
al.

"I suggested we go meet them," Frank said. "When
you're on a high you can be perfect and act perfectly too.
So I went into each complex and got a commitment from
all those people for $800,000."

From there, Frank went to some wealthy people he
knew might help him, some of them old friends from his
childhood. He made a lot of phone calls, pushed and bad-
gered a lot of people and set up a meeting for Saturday
morning with the shop owners.

He thought he was about to put the deal together, but
Joanne, seeing that he was totally out of control, refused
to agree to it. She was so frightened by the high he was on
that she spent a night in a motel to get away from him.

Thursday night Frank barged into the home of a relative, insisted he was the Holy Spirit, then left. By Friday
morning Joanne was trying to find a mental hospital that
would take him. She got a room, but Frank refused to go.

Saturday morning she called their lawyer, told him

about the situation and canceled the meeting. On Sunday afternoon, Joanne said, Frank went to his room, began playing with his pills and threatened to kill himself, or harm her.

"I was absolutely shocked," she said. "I was so petrified I picked up my purse and left."

Monday morning Joanne signed a mental inquest warrant so that the police could arrest her husband. Before that could happen, though, Frank signed himself into a mental hospital, signed himself out, returned Monday afternoon to sign himself in again, then left again.

The police arrested him at a relative's house Monday night. He was placed on the back-seat floor of the police car. He was taken to the mental hospital and placed in a lock-up ward where he preached for about five hours.

Frank Marx had no control over any of this. He had been given drugs over the years, but they did not solve the problem, a problem in his brain that robbed him of any control. He still hadn't been diagnosed as a manic-depressive.

He was in the hospital a month. His weight dropped from 235 pounds to 186 pounds. He was given Haldol, which helped bring him off the high, but it took a long time to be effective. Even when he was released and went home, he did not feel much better. He couldn't relax. He'd stay in bed six or eight hours a day playing the same tape over and over — a tape that was supposed to help him relax.

"I drove Joanne nuts," he said. "I must have played it 10 or 15 times a day."

Still unhappy, Frank attended a 12-step, self-help program at the suggestion of a family friend. There he met a man who suggested that Frank see a psychiatrist who might help him. The man — who Frank had only known three days — paid the $1,000 registration fee that was required to have Frank re-admitted to the mental hospital where the psychiatrist worked. The psychiatrist immediately diagnosed him as manic-depressive.

Frank was given Tegretol to level out his moods but was not a changed man immediately.

"After about five days I got very angry and I started giving the doctor a lot of hell," he said. "The doctor said, 'OK, I'm not going to take care of you anymore' and quit. He said, 'I've had it. Nobody talks to me like you talked to me.' "

For several days after that Frank had difficulty finding any doctor who would deal with him. Then the doctor who had walked out on him came back, saying that he had taken an oath to his patients and he would stick by it.

Frank straightened up.

"I told him I'd do what he wanted," Frank said. "We've been friends ever since."

Once calmed down, Frank was given a combination of lithium and Tegretol. He went back to the hospital briefly in 1986, but mostly has continued his life as a parent, husband and chemical salesman. He has been to the racetrack only four or five times in the last five years.

He knows it was Joanne who kept their company going while he was ill. After awhile, with the new drugs working, Frank was able to function well enough to resume selling chemicals while Joanne did the books.

"I don't know how we saved the company," she said. "The fact we didn't lose it is a miracle."

But Joanne's help went beyond the business. She learned of a national self-help program for manic-depressives and depressives. She and Frank attended a meeting in Washington, D.C., then returned to Louisville to begin a similar organization here. By helping hundreds of other people with similar problems, they have better learned to understand each other.

"I'll tell you what," she said. "I was brought up with six brothers in a family where everybody worked hard. You lived through whatever it was and you didn't complain.

"But when all this was over and it looked like we were going to survive, and the company was all right, then it was just 'God bless America!' I started thinking about how I felt. I had never thought about myself. It was always my kids. It was always Frank, and what am I going to do with him?

"So I got some help. I said I wasn't going to take this anymore. When we started this manic-depressive association I learned theories of detaching and letting go. And that I deserve to be happy, and I can't always make him happy. I feel a whole lot better about myself."

The Marxes' oldest son, Frank III, 26, said he was certainly aware of his father's illness, his moodiness and occasional rages, but their relationship suffered no long-term trauma.

"He would get what I call out-of-line angry," Frank III said, "really bent out of shape over things that were fairly trivial. At that point — I was like 12 or 13 — I don't know if I would have attributed them to the illness or just a difference in perspective.

"The truth is, for the most part, my father has been a really compelling figure in my life. A real role model, really. He's got all the things in a role model that I really value; he's high-energy, he's focused, he's driven.

"I think in that he has committed to try to be self-maintaining with his illness, it's really helped our relationship.

He's open about it. I know he's trying to do something
about it by starting this self-help group. When
he feels an episode coming on, he knows what to do. He's
made a commitment to deal with his illness, and he's
done it really well."

Frank's younger brother, Joe, 24, lives in Washington,
D.C. He said that when he was young he was sometimes
reluctant to bring friends to the house because his father
was so moody.

"I think they felt awkward and very uncomfortable,"
he said.

Joe also said it was his mother who absorbed a lot of
the shock from his father's illness, who made it much eas-
ier for him to live at home, especially during the adolescent years.

But Joe, too, has love and respect for his father, as a
role model, as the man who encouraged him to be the
best and backed it up with college-tuition payments, as a
figure who was there when it counted.

"I think my father has had a very rough life and has
done incredibly well with what he had to work with," Joe
said. "He was very positive and very supportive."

Mr. Frank Marx Jr.
1100 Ambridge Drive
Louisville, Kentucky 40207

Dear Frank,

You are to be commended, my dear friend, for your unbounded enthusiasm and determination to establish a halfway house in Louisville for persons suffering from manic-depression and depression to assist them in making the transition from a hospital setting to a regular work-home setting.

Yours is indeed a timely and worthwhile goal since more and more we read of the economic and competitive effects of depression on the nations' workforce and workplace. If businesses in the United States and in our community are to be fully competitive in the markets of the 1990s, we will need all available workers working at their maximum efficiency.

How well aware are you, too, Frank, of the critical need for sheltered rehabilitation and housing for such persons to support them in their healing process. A halfway facility provides help to the many individuals who do not have a strong and dedicated circle of family and friends.

I wish you all the best success in you endeavors. If I can ever be of assistance in this or any other matter, please do not hesitate to let me know.

With all best wishes and warmest personal regards.

Sincerely,
Romano L. Mazzoli
Member of Congress

The Manic Depressive and Depressive Association of
Louisville Inc.
P.O. Box 7315
Louisville, Kentucky 40257-0315


Dear Association
   It is a pleasure to take part in your organization's effort
to establish a halfway house for person with manic-
depressive and depressive disorders. Your proposed
halfway house has vast potential for long-range contributions to mental health for all Kentuckians.
   I congratulate the members of your organization for the
help you have already accorded the patients and their
families with these disorders. A halfway house facility
would be yet another important phase in the treatment
of patients with these psychological problems.
   I hope the establishment of this halfway house
becomes a reality  because it signifies progress and the
realization of the dreams of dedicated people.
   Through your organization's perseverance, the halfway
house could be a milestone in  our state's long struggle
against mental illness.

Sincerely,
Bert T. Combs

One of Kentucky's greatest needs for its citizens suffering from mental illness is transitional residential and supported housing. Not unlike persons suffering from debilitating physical illnesses, their needs are essentially the same: a continuity of care which is accessible, appropriate and affordable.

This translates into careful, professional diagnosis, a proper treatment plan and follow-up care. All too often Kentucky's mentally ill have difficulty in accessing appropriate continuity of care, and if they are successful, the third vital link toward recovery is usually missing; that is, transitional and/or sustained residential facilities geared to meet their needs.

It is not enough to identify and treat a patient if recovery is the expected result. These persons suffering from schizophrenia, manic-depression and related depressive disorders usually cannot maintain their medication regime as well as trying to regain or maintain their skills without a stable family or a residential facility to enable them to receive continuing support in a caring environment.

Your association's recognition of the unmet need and its dedication to face this challenge is commendable and is evidence of caring and inspired leadership.

I wish you every success in establishing a transitional residential facility for persons with manic-depressive and depressive disorders.

God bless and good luck.

Cornelia A. Serpell
Mental Health Advocate

Mood disorders are classified into two groups: those with just depression and those with both highs and lows (called manic-depressive, or the newer term, bipolar). Various estimates of prevalence have been made. Ballpark figures from the National Institute of Mental Health are that 5.8 percent of our population has a depression during any given six-month period. Depression is the most common illness there is. Its severity, duration and varieties of physical and mental symptoms vary widely. It is not a single disorder but a group of disorders. It can be most incapacitating, and even lethal. It often exists in a cloud of shame and guilt. It is one of the most painful experiences of mankind. Its costs in personal misery, loss of quality of life, economic loss and damage to family functioning are staggering.

Both of these illnesses are "brain diseases" and are not due to personal or character weaknesses. It is most inaccurate to label these as "chemical imbalances," a currently favorite pop phrase. They are correctly seen as biopsychosocial, meaning that biological, psychological and environmental factors combine in various ways and degrees to impact on brain functioning. Heredity plays a partial role in some. Some are triggered by stress, others come out of the blue, a few are triggered by the seasonal changes in sunlight. These disorders come in the form of episodes interspersed with normal states, but a small percentage can become chronic.

Eighty-five percent to 90 percent respond favorably to appropriate treatment. Unfortunately, some physicians mismanage these. When patients are not responding it is useful to get a second opinion from a psychiatrist not associated with the attending physician.

Mood disturbances vary in degree and duration and are sometimes fluctuating over time. Presently only two settings are available for their care, home or hospital. An intermediate facility, such as a halfway house, is needed for those who are too sick to be at home yet not sick enough to meet the current criteria for hospitalization.

Patients at a halfway house would stay only as long as their condition warranted. They would care for themselves. All would be under the care of a psychiatrist, and all psychiatrists on the staff would be approved by the medical advisory committee.

Mr. Frank Marx, the president of the Louisville Chapter of the Manic Depressive and Depressive Association, approached the undersigned a few years ago with the proposition that a halfway house was needed. All who have examined the concept have agreed. Halfway houses are the cutting edge in modern technology for many psychiatric disorders. A whole spectrum of treatment factors — facilities, team personnel, medications, psychotherapy, family counseling, environmental changes, research — has proven effective, when orchestrated by competent professionals.

The true stories contained herein are not written primarily to underscore the need for a halfway house, but for readers to understand these disorders a bit more, assist in destigmatization of mental illness and spark sympathetic and empathetic caring. There but for the grace of God could go any of us. We can thank those who have courageously shared their experiences with us.

Harvey R. St. Clair, M.D.
Chair, Medical Advisory Committee
Manic Depressive and Depressive Association

Mr. Frank W. Marx, Jr.
President and Executive Director

The Manic Depressive
and Depressive Association of Louisville
P. O. Box 7315
Louisville, Kentucky 40207


Dear Mr. Marx,

I think your proposal for a halfway house for those suffering from depression or manic-depression is a very
good one.

One of our society's major problems today is the lack of
suitable facilities for those who no longer need intensive
treatment in a mental hospital, but who need support,
rehabilitation and resocialization while recovering from
episodes or relapses of their illness.

Cyclical illnesses, such as manic-depression and depression, would especially benefit from such a halfway house.

Since studies have shown the therapeutic value for all
people of working with animals, the combination of a
halfway house and horse farm, is also an excellent idea.

The need for halfway houses for those with mental illnesses in our community and all communities is great.

Too many former mental patients fall between the
cracks, taking a toll on their families, and themselves.
Homelessness or hopelessness is often the result.

A halfway house, such as you propose, might have
averted these results.

But in any case, no society can be truly great which does
not offer compassionate care for those suffering from
mental illnesses.

A halfway house would provide such care, and we

would be grateful to have it in Jefferson County.

Sincerely,

David L. Armstrong
Jefferson County Judge/Executive

The Manic Depressive
and Depressive Association
P. O. Box 7315
Louisville, Kentucky 40205


Gentlemen:

I have met with Frank Marx and we have discussed his
idea for a halfway house for the rehabilitation of manic-
depressive and depressive patients. Mr. Marx's idea of
basing treatment around the atmosphere and background
of a horse farm, is, I feel, an excellent one. We have discussed the fact that, although there will be a majority of
patients able to pay for their treatment, there will also be
some that will be unable to handle the cost. This is why
Mr. Marx has approached me with the idea of horse owners donating animals to the program.

The animals, thoroughbred horses, in particular would
be used to generate income for the farm. They can be sold
as in-foal mares, or bred, and the resulting offspring sold
as weanlings or yearlings. This income would then be
used to help cover the costs of treatment for those
patients unable to pay for their own treatment.

Regarding the donation of these animals, it should be
made clear that this will not be a retirement home for animals that are no longer useful, such as geldings, infertile
mares and stallions. The animals donated would be
appraised at a fair market value and treated as any other
donation to a non-profit organization.

I realize that the real challenge is in acquiring these
donations, however, I feel that there are many people in
the thoroughbred industry that will be willing to make
donations of this kind. Mr. Marx has a good idea and if I

can be of any further assistance, please do not hesitate to contact me.


Sincerely,
William D. Wright
Farm Consultant
Paris, Kentucky

Subject: Residence Building for MDDA

The structure is to be a two-story, motel-type structure designed to accommodate up to 152 guests. The construction is to be concrete block with brick veneer exterior walls and steel stud with drywall for all interior walls except for fire walls. Heating ventilation and air conditioning is to be done by individual room units with the common areas serviced by drop-in roof units. The structure and parking facilities will require a minimum of three (3) acres of ground.

| | |
|---|---:|
| First floor square footage | 24,200 |
| Second floor square footage | 23,184 |
| Individual rooms | 152 |
| Individual rooms square footage | |
| Bedroom | 136 |
| Bathroom | 35 |
| Storage and utility square footage | 1,269 |
| Laundry room square footage | 315 |

The building also contains the following:

Eight (8) kitchen areas
Five (5) lounge areas
Administrator's apartment
One (1) consultation room
Five (5) public men's and women's toilets
Pool and garden area

Estimated cost is based on motel construction costs of approximately $71.80 per square foot. $3,402,000.

Estimated architect's fee is 7% or $238,000.

Cost of land to be added.

Contributions are now being accepted to establish a fund for a halfway house to be operated by the Manic Depressive and Depressive Association of Louisville, Inc.The Please send donations to:
Manic Depressive and Depressive Association
of Louisville, Inc.
P. O. Box 7315
Louisville, Kentucky 40257-0315

Your donation is deductible to the full extent allowed by law.

Thank you